MONEY MADE EASY

Paul Merriman, aka askpaul, is one of Ireland's leading financial advisors. With an internationally recognised CFP® certification and over twenty years' experience in the financial sector, Paul began his financial life in RSA and Irish Life before launching askpaul, a jargon-free financial advice service, in 2016.

In 2023, askpaul became part of Fairstone with Paul currently CEO of Fairstone Ireland. Paul regularly appears on television and radio to share his straight-talking, no-nonsense advice and expert tips on all things finance.

MONEY MADE EASY

SIMPLE STEPS TO MANAGING YOUR FINANCES

Paul Merriman

HACHETTE
BOOKS
IRELAND

First published in Ireland in 2024 by
HACHETTE BOOKS IRELAND

2

Cataloguing in Publication Data is available from the British Library.

ISBN 9781399730822

Typeset in Adobe Caslon Pro by Bookends Publishing Services, Dublin
Printed and bound in Great Britain by Clays Ltd, Elcograf S.p.A.

The infographic used in the Mortgages section is kindly reproduced with permission from First Home Scheme (firsthomescheme.ie); the mortgage repayment tables are kindly produced with permission from the Competition and Consumer Protection Commission's website using its money tool (ccpc.ie); the graphics of the risk check calculator are kindly reproduced with permission from Aviva (aviva.ie); the loan calculator is kindly reproduced with permission from Credit Union (creditunion.ie); information provided courtesy of the Revenue Commissioners under a Creative Commons Attribution 4.0 International (CC BY 4.0) licence

Hachette Books Ireland policy is to use papers that are natural, renewable and recyclable products and made from wood grown in sustainable forests. The logging and manufacturing processes are expected to conform to the environmental regulations of the country of origin.

Hachette Books Ireland
8 Castlecourt Centre
Castleknock
Dublin 15, Ireland

A division of Hachette UK Ltd
Carmelite House, 50 Victoria Embankment, London EC4Y 0DZ
www.hachettebooksireland.ie

This book is dedicated to my amazing family:

To my wife Sarah, thank you always for
your constant love and support.

To our children, Cian, Charli, Luca and Archie,
thank you for all the fun and laughter, and
know everything I do is for you and your future.

To Mam, Maureen, and Dad, Paul, the original 'askpaul',
thank you for all the sacrifices you made as I grew up.

CONTENTS

Section 1 **Personal Budgeting**

Section 2 **Managing Your Debt**

Section 3 **Saving and Investing**

Section 4 **Tax**

Section 5 **Financial Protection**

Section 6 **Mortgages**

Section 7 **Pensions**

FINANCIAL PLANNING
LET'S GET STARTED

What is a financial planner?

My job as a financial planner is to make my clients financially secure.

It's not very complicated. When you come in to see me, we sit down, have a conversation and I find out where you want to get to. I analyse your situation and, using various metrics, forecast your finances until you're a hundred. Then, I create a plan to secure your future.

I find out what your goals and hopes are – and what your responsibilities are. Then, I identify any gaps or weaknesses in the existing plan. When I've helped you identify your financial goals, we create a roadmap to achieve them.

However, financial planning is not a one-off event. It's an ongoing process that involves regular monitoring and adjustments. I like to review plans yearly to ensure they're still aligned with clients' goals. Then, I'll make adjustments based on changes in their circumstances or the broader financial landscape.

This book will show you how to establish what you want from a financial plan. Having a plan is a great achievement in itself and will focus your mind on managing your money better.

When do I need a financial planner?

As I will explain, getting a financial plan together is not that complex. It takes a little time, but creating the plan is the easy part. It gets more complicated at the next stage – navigating tax implications, legal issues, inheritance, pension legislation, all the finer technicalities of investing.

Yes, I will explain many of the basics of these issues here. I'll keep it simple but, by the end of this book, you'll have a good understanding of stocks, shares, equities and investment funds. And you'll have a solid grounding in budgets and pensions, personal tax and protecting your assets. This will all help you to make informed decisions regarding your finances.

However, it's impossible to cover everyone's very individual circumstances and, sometimes, making long-term financial commitments can be a legislative quagmire.

It takes years of experience to know your way around this maze and a lot of work to stay on top of constantly changing tax rules and legislation. When you reach that next level when you're considering what to do with a lump sum or starting a pension, that's when you may need to see a financial planner. If you have concerns about making your next move, seek the guidance of a good financial planner. If you have any doubts or confusion, please look before you leap and seek professional advice.

The most important benefit of financial planning is the peace of mind that comes with having that plan and making informed decisions.

Who am I?

My name is Paul Merriman. I was born and raised in Tallaght in Dublin, and now I live in Foxrock with my wife Sarah and our four children.

I am the Irish CEO of Fairstone Asset Management DAC and a shareholder in Fairstone in Ireland, home to the financial-planning advice site askpaul.ie, based in Stillorgan in Dublin. With my talented team (currently ninety-three people), my company looks after more than 15,000 clients acrossIreland and by the end of 2024 will manage €1 billion in assets.

How did I start in finance?

For me, an obsession with finances began earlier than most – as a seven-year-old kid. I remember sitting at the kitchen table, looking up at my father and brother-in-law, David, chatting about business. They were all involved in the construction industry, and I sat there wide-eyed, gazing from one to the other, fascinated by the exchanges and business chat.

'Did you hear who got the tender for the school extensions?'

'What about Ryan's going to the wall?'

'You better change that quote again – the price of plasterboard has gone through the roof.'

'We still haven't received payment for that job.'

'The tender for that job will be ready next week …'

It sounds odd, but I was hooked by the chatter about pricing jobs, managing budgets and cash flow – though not hooked enough to join my family and work in the construction industry. I was a sickly child, in and out of Temple Street and Crumlin hospitals for operations to deal with a kidney complaint. I even completed some of my Junior Cert. in Temple Street Hospital.

I still have kidney issues and will probably be on dialysis before I reach sixty. But I feel lucky that I'm aware of it and can plan for it. I know I must enjoy life in my forties and fifties because I'll possibly be tied to dialysis three times a week in my sixties. I've seen clients suddenly suffer a major illness in their fifties or sixties and be derailed by it. So, I kind of feel lucky that I know what's coming. I can make sure I'm financially secure.

I like to say my family dissuaded me from the physicality of the building industry because of my medical issues, but they'd probably turn around and say I was too lazy to get into the trade. Let's say the truth lies somewhere in the middle.

I completed the Leaving Cert. the year that Y2K was supposed to end the world and 'Maniac 2000' topped the charts. The turn of the century was an optimistic time in Ireland. The country was experiencing real economic growth and the frenzy of selling each other property in the early 2000s was only starting. Even though my interest in all things financial was high, my knowledge was low and I had no clear career path ahead of me.

Somebody told me computers were the future, so I went to college to study electrical engineering. But the first lecture might as well have been in Swahili for all I understood. I was out of my depth and left just after Rag Week. I didn't dare tell my dad, though. I got a job in Dunnes Stores' off-licence in The Square shopping centre in Tallaght and pretended I went to college every day. I changed into my Dunnes' uniform in their toilets.

How did I start a career as a financial planner?

After three months working in the off-licence, my mother showed me an advert for a job in the general insurance company Royal Sun Alliance (RSA). Dad still thinks I left college to start work in RSA on 20 January 2001. (Sorry, Dad)

RSA was a vast and vibrant company filled with young employees like me. I worked in the Dawson Street offices and, being a teenager, loved being based in the city centre.

My brain is wired to be a spender rather than a saver. It always seemed easier to me to earn €5,000 than save it. Around this time, I thought about taking time off to travel to Australia. My salary in RSA wouldn't have stretched to funding my nights out *and* an extended holiday in Australia, which is when my entrepreneurial side kicked in. I figured if I worked nights and weekends, I'd have enough cash to survive a few months in Australia. So, I took a second job delivering pizza for Dominos.

I put my head down, worked all the hours I could get and got a nice lump sum together. I'd seen my older siblings doing this when buying their first houses. It was about knuckling down, working all the hours I could and minimising my spending. I was twenty years old, and this was the first sign of an inner financial planner emerging from within me. However, I didn't make it to Australia – the money went to buy a car instead – but I did like the feeling of earning and working out how to make money work for me.

Budgeting and sensible money management didn't come to me for a couple of years, though. That transformation began at twenty-two when my first child, Cian, was born. The power and influence of a tiny baby is amazing. Suddenly, I felt pressure to succeed and the urge to be a good provider. After three years in RSA, I decided I needed to earn more money. So, I applied for a better-paying position as a junior financial planner with Irish Life & Permanent. After a couple of attempts, I got a job with Irish Life despite my inexperience and, in 2005, found myself in months of intensive training in the Abbey Street offices. It was a top-class education.

They gave us a DVD (yes, a DVD), and that introduction to financial planning instilled a love for our profession that remains with me to this day. I remember the sleeve it came in, taking it out and watching it at home hundreds of times, mesmerised.

It featured a general manager in Irish Life, Paddy Finnegan (a legend in business and now the CEO of Mercedes Ireland), explaining the concept of financial advising. He spoke about what the job entailed and how we could help people achieve their goals in life.

I'm still not sure exactly what inspired me, but I think it was the realisation that this could be the start of a real career rather than just a job. I also knew it could be financially rewarding and, as a new dad, I felt that pressure to succeed.

Everything about the career appealed to me. I had been searching for a path and, as I watched that DVD, I found it. Watching that video lit a fire in me and nothing has ever extinguished those flames. It was like I'd found my vocation in life. I decided I wanted to be nothing else but a financial planner. This may seem like a weird statement – there aren't many people who dream of being a financial planner – but that DVD and how Paddy spoke inspired me to believe I could make an impact in people's lives.

I always remember one of my first clients was a couple, the Cummins. On my first visit to their house, their eldest, Sean, was having his Debs night. I'm proud to say that after all these years, the Cummins are still clients of mine – and so are their sons.

And that's one of the beauties of financial planning to me. You get to connect with people on a different level. You learn about a client's family and children, their hopes for the future, their dreams and goals. Connecting with people makes this profession unique. You build lifelong relationships and impact countless lives, and people are genuinely appreciative when you help them. I find my job rewarding beyond measure.

Those years working in Irish Life coincided with the last roars of the Celtic Tiger, the name given to Ireland's economic boom from 2000 to 2007. When I started, my salary was €40,000, and I had all the status symbols – the company car, the phone and the laptop. It was more than I had ever earned before. I brimmed with confidence I'd told them at the interview that I wanted to make €90,000 within a year. I surprised the company by earning approximately €100,000 in my second year with commissions on sales.

The money I earned got crazy as 2008 approached (see below). Everyone was investing in property, so it was all about getting mortgages for clients. Then, we sold life assurance on top of mortgages. People had a lot of money to invest, so there was a lot of activity in the market.

What was the global financial crash of 2008?

It all began when Lehman Brothers, one of the biggest and oldest investment banks in America, went bankrupt in September 2008. Why? In the early 2000s, America experienced a huge housing boom like other countries around the world, including Ireland. Lehman Brothers jumped onto the bandwagon, investing heavily in 'subprime mortgages'. Subprime mortgages are loans given to people who might struggle to pay them back.

However, the bank made a risky bet that didn't pay off. The glut of money in the housing market led to a rush of house construction in the U.S. But eventually, they built too many houses, and supply outstripped demand. The housing market in America began to nosedive, and a domino effect began. Homeowners started defaulting on their mortgage payments. This meant companies, like Lehman, who had invested heavily in these mortgages, started losing money – lots of it. To make matters worse, Lehman had borrowed a lot of money to invest, magnifying their losses as the economy declined.

Investors got nervous and withdrew their investments. An attempt to sell the bank failed. They didn't have the advantage of a government bailout, so they had to declare bankruptcy in September 2008.

There's a popular saying: when America sneezes, the rest of the world catches a cold. The domino effect continued into global markets, marking the beginning of a worldwide financial crisis.

The shockwaves reached all the way to Ireland. Until the 2008 crash, Ireland had an extraordinary party going on. Our dramatic financial growth was known as the Celtic Tiger economy, and the tiger was roaring by 2006 and 2007. Property prices were skyrocketing, and banks offered cheap loans to anyone who wanted money to invest in the lucrative market. When Lehman Brothers collapsed, the music stopped and Ireland was plunged into a global financial crisis.

Just like Lehman Brothers, Irish banks had borrowed heavily from international banks to fund the property spree. Banks around the world stopped lending to each other and credit dried up. As the property market crashed, non-repayments soared, and the banks became in danger of collapsing.

The Irish government came rushing to the rescue amid fears of mass deposit withdrawals. They gave an unconditional guarantee to cover the debts of Irish banks, but at an enormous cost to everyone in the country.

It led to a significant increase in public debt, and Ireland, in turn, ended up needing an €85 billion bailout from the EU and International Monetary Fund in 2010. The aftershocks of the crisis were huge. The building industry collapsed, thousands lost their jobs, many lost their homes, emigration and taxes soared. The government even raided private pensions to raise funds.

They introduced a controversial measure termed a 'pension levy' in 2011 which deducted money from private pension funds.

The levy, applied at a rate of 0.6% per annum on the market value of assets, was extended until 2015.

The financial crisis was like a tremendous storm which left its mark on the Irish landscape, and we're still cleaning up the mess today. Memories of the crisis have influenced attitudes. I've seen many clearing their debts since, and people generally have a more cautious approach to borrowing and spending. The crisis highlighted the importance of responsible financial management versus the rampant consumerism and borrowing we saw in the early 2000s.

Back to me, again. I watched the economy go into freefall, and the national mood going from buoyant to despairing.

I was still young, so the crash didn't affect me too severely. I'm blessed that I hadn't joined Irish Life two or three years earlier because I might have been up to my neck in property deals if I had. Instead, my money went on my first home and a big mortgage. I never got involved in other property deals or syndicates. I didn't buy investment properties.

However, I did the 'responsible' thing and invested in bank shares and employee shares in Irish Life & Permanent. The shares vaporised, which was an early lesson in diversification. (We'll discuss this later.) My house went into negative equity. My salary plunged as everyone stopped investing and the mortgage market stopped abruptly. It felt like the world was ending – overnight, Ireland became a new country.

The financial news seemed to worsen daily, but I remember the philosophical attitude of one of the investment managers, Seán Haverty. 'This will just bounce back,' he said. 'It's going to be the same as every other crash.'

I shook my head. 'No, this is different. Like, this is the worst market crash since the Great Depression in 1929.'

The Great Depression and the Wall Street stock-market crash was an economic shock that affected most countries across the world from 1929 and right through the 1930s. But that crash was something I'd read about – this one was real, and it felt horrendous.

But Seán was right – the markets did bounce back and people started to do deals again by 2011 and 2012.

When the COVID-19 pandemic struck in 2020, it was a tragedy on a human level, but it also seemed like another global financial disaster. I remember sitting at my desk fretting: 'This is different. This is going to be a shit show. This is going to be the end of the world. Economies are locking down. People are dying. We've never seen this before. This is Armageddon.'

Then, I remembered what Seán had told me all those years earlier and I took a deep breath. At first, the markets were down but then, three months later, boom! Tech stocks started flying. Everyone was watching Netflix, taking Zoom calls and shopping online, and the economy was rolling again. Money always finds its way to the top.

I saw the 2008 crash wipe out many people financially. It was a complete disaster but also a valuable learning curve at the start of my career. I learned that when things go wrong, it doesn't last for ever. Economies and stock markets rebound quickly. Most of all, I learned from other people's mistakes – mistakes that I try to absorb for our clients going forward.

Anyway, let's get back to the early days of the crash when I was still working in Irish Life. The head office was in Abbey Street in Dublin, but I was in the Stillorgan sales office. One morning, I arrived early, before any of my colleagues, and found a notice in my post box. The notice said that the Life Insurance Association (LIA) was introducing the Certified Financial Planner (CFP®) qualification in Ireland.

The certification is the standard of excellence in financial planning. It was a step beyond the standard Qualified Financial Advisor (QFA) and I was immediately interested. Places were limited. The Irish Life senior management team still considered me a junior, so I worried that they would overlook my application for someone who'd been in the role longer than me. So, luckily for me, I was the first in the office that morning, before 7am, and I was therefore first to submit my application and I got the course. The early bird catches the worm. I suppose I gave management no choice but to approve it.

Education did what it was supposed to – it broadened my horizons and aspirations. I took my qualification as a CFP® seriously. I wanted to empower clients and help them achieve their goals. But the course also taught me that I could never put my clients' interests first because Irish Life was a 'tied agency'. Tied agents can only sell their company's products and, in my opinion, you can't fulfil your duty as a financial planner when you're tied to one company. I feel it's not ethical.

I realised financial brokers offered products from across the whole of the market, so they had greater fund choices for their clients. The brokering sector now holds 76% market share of all financial planning. Financial brokers are often QFAs and when a client comes looking for a pension, for example, they will typically advise them on the right product. Whereas a CFP®'s primary role is financial planning. If a client comes to me looking for a pension, I take an overview of their whole financial situation first. Products like pensions only follow when I've devised a financial plan for the client. CFP®s and QFAs are different.

I decided it was time to go out on my own and set up my own financial-planning business, so I left Irish Life. I worked briefly in a financial brokerage, setting up their life and pension division. Then I bought out a brokerage called Pax Asset Management in 2011.

As a Facebook user, I had come across a social-media guru in America named Gary Vaynerchuk, known as Gary Vee. He talked about people bringing their passion to the wider market through social media. He had a book – *AskGaryVee* – which gave me the idea for askpaul.

In 2016, under Central Bank of Ireland authorisation, I founded and launched the askpaul brand as part of Pax Asset Management.

With Gary Vee's influence, I started carving my own niche in the financial-services market in Ireland. I became one of the first in the industry to develop a social-media presence on platforms like YouTube, Facebook and Snapchat.

My first video was horrendous. It took my nephew Daniel and me eight hours to record, even though it's about thirty seconds long. This calamity is still online, and I'm strangely proud of it because it reminds me of how far we've come. (Check out that first video on the askpaul YouTube channel.)

Despite that inauspicious start, we produced many nuggets of content. The aim was always the same – to help people unravel personal finance, interest rates, mortgages, pensions and taxes.

The first video that blew up was taken when I was on holiday in Madrid, and I compared banks in Spain to banks in Ireland. It was the first time we got 100,000-plus views.

Soon, the social-media strategy began to work. It was like magic. Really quickly, I started being asked to appear on television and radio. One of my first radio slots was on Dublin's Q102, and I'm still on the air with them every Wednesday morning. I regularly contribute to Virgin Media, Today FM and Newstalk. In six years, we went from twelve staff to sixty-six and from hundreds of clients to more than 10,000 clients.

Our jargon-free advice struck a chord with people, and we now have a huge online audience. Hundreds of thousands of people watch our free advice and on-demand webinars. By giving straight advice in layman's terms, we have gone from strength to strength. We also have tens of thousands signed up to the askpaul newsletter on www.askpaul.ie.

Our rapid growth attracted the attention of Fairstone, one of the largest wealth management firms in the UK, when they were looking to partner with a firm in Ireland. I sold Pax Asset Management to Fairstone in 2022 and I am now the Irish CEO of Fairstone Asset Management DAC. We aim to build on their strengths and experience in the UK to further our goals of making financial planning a norm in Irish society.

Why the DIY approach to planning often fails

As I've said, the most important benefit of financial planning is the peace of mind that comes with having that plan. You work hard for your money, and it should work hard for you, providing the security you need in unplanned emergencies.

Some of you will read this book and make a successful and comprehensive financial plan. Some of you will actually follow that plan. For the rest of you, having an active professional looking over your shoulder may help keep you accountable. Some people need that 'gentle' nudge to stay on track with their plan.

The DIY approach can backfire in other ways too. I see many efforts to be financially prudent that don't work. I've listed below examples of well-intentioned behaviours that are actually counterproductive.

ACTION	ISSUE
The client has a pension plan and is funding an additional voluntary contribution.	The same client is still living at home with his parents. He should invest in his life now first and save for a house.
The client puts regular monthly savings for a long-term goal into a deposit account.	These accounts earn little to no interest. A savings plan that invests in growing assets, such as equities, bonds and/or commodities, makes more sense.
The client is insuring his €1,000 smartphone for €15 a month in perpetuity.	He should insure his income which bought the phone. The smartphone insurance money would contribute significantly to a monthly policy insuring his income.
The client left a pension pot with an old employer, assuming it is well managed.	Poor investment performance was hindering the growth of the fund he left behind.

CLIENT CASE
PATRICK, AGED 45

Business owner Patrick planned to sell his business in a few years. He had a pension plan and came to us to make a significant top-up to his pension.

Instead, we advised Patrick to hold off on the pension. He could take cash out of the business in a more tax-efficient way than a pension by using the Entrepreneurial Relief Scheme. When a person qualifies, this relief reduces Capital Gains Tax from 33% to 10% on the first €1 million of qualifying assets.

This is an example of how financial planning works in favour of the client rather than the finance company. Selling a big pension would have been great for our company. However, it served Patrick's interests better to hold off on increasing his pension until a later date.

Who uses a financial planner?

Anyone can benefit from using a financial planner.

We work with many high-net-worth individuals, such as those selling their businesses and looking for tax-efficient exit strategies. That's a big focus of our practice and we have many clients in that area. Other clients first come to our offices when they want to buy a house, retire, start a business or some other significant life event.

But we help people at all stages of life with every income. Some want to set up education funds using their children's allowance or make small investments or take out income-protection policies. People from every walk of life use financial planners.

Where can I find a financial planner?

My advice is to contact askpaul.ie. I may be biased, but the team there is the best in the business. They're all lovely people – especially the boss!

Alternatively, see the list of financial planners on the Financial Planning Standards Board Ireland's website (www. fpsb.ie). People with problem debt can also contact the Money Advice and Budgeting Service (MABS; https://mabs.ie). This is a terrific service offering free and independent advice and support.

People can also start their financial journey by brushing up their own knowledge. Lots of financial advice is available for free. Askpaul has a free virtual academy on our website, and it's available to everybody, whether you live on social welfare or have millions. We answer direct messages on our Instagram page and answer thousands of emails. I'm up sometimes until 2 a.m. replying to direct messages from people who are not even clients.

Whatever expert advisor you choose, it's vital that you like your financial planner. You need to build a personal, ongoing relationship and you need to trust them. It's not just a transaction-based process: 'I want a pension.' 'I want a mortgage.' It should be: 'I want to work on my financial plan over the next few decades. Can you help me?' That's what a financial planner should be doing.

I recommend interviewing multiple planners and asking for references from their clients. We introduce anyone nervous about advice or investment to other clients with similar circumstances.

When do I use a financial planner?

The best time to use a financial planner is when you start earning an income. That's how you'll get the greatest benefits from the process.

Usually, we meet clients for the first time when they are involved in a major life event, such as buying a house, retiring, or starting/selling a business. Sometimes, unfortunately, we only see them for the first time when they are already in trouble.

But financial planning is *not* just for retiring or the big-ticket events in life. It should be an ongoing process throughout your adult life. If you're starting to save, invest money or change jobs, please take financial advice. Ditto for taking redundancy, getting married, starting a family, buying a house or planning retirement. Your income provides all your wealth and resources in this life (unless you inherit money). Look after it.

How much does a financial planner cost?

Financial planners in Ireland have different ways of charging clients. The typical payment model for financial planners in the United States, Canada and Australia is fee-based. However, fee-based systems never took off here because the typical cost of a complete financial plan is around €2,500, and few Irish consumers will pay that. So only a few financial planners work on a fee base in Ireland.

Typically, financial brokers give a free financial plan and use the renumeration structure from any products sold to the client to pay for the service. Others use a combination of hourly rates and policy fees on any products purchased.

Our company, like many, goes for a hybrid system with an upfront fee – typically €250 – and commission on any products sold. Sometimes, we have promotional offers so there are no fees or reduced fees to work on your financial plan.

Of course, there needs to be a high level of integrity in creating a financial plan when commissions are part of the fee structure. Maintaining client trust is crucial. All financial planners must adhere to the Central Bank's *Consumer Protection Code* (CPC). The first principle of which is that we must act in a customer's best interests.

Everyone in our company has a duty to the clients to provide unbiased and transparent advice. After all, reputation and trustworthiness are essential in this relationship-based business. A good reputation leads to client loyalty, more referrals and sustainable business growth.

The cost of using financial planners usually pays for itself many times over. Planners pursue the most economical and tax-efficient means to navigate complex financial matters. We make sure you make the most of your money and avoid pitfalls that can cost you thousands.

CLIENT CASE
JOÃO & LILIAN, AGED 43 & 41

My role is to look out for the client's best interests, and sometimes that means discouraging them from buying products that are not right for them.

João and Lilian wanted to make additional voluntary contributions to their pension recently. Yes, it was tax efficient and seemed the right thing to do, but they already had two very well-funded pensions.

They were astonished when I suggested adding the money to their living expenses rather than making more contributions.

They had two young children and had worked hard, so I suggested they take more holiday time for once instead of doing the financially sensible thing.

It seemed counterintuitive to them but, eventually, they came around. Instead of using their wealth to overfund life in their eighties, they decided it was the right time to enjoy it now with their kids.

Putting more money in their pension was tax efficient, but it wasn't life-enhancing. There's a balance to be struck sometimes.

THE PATH TO
FINANCIAL WELL-BEING

I've been a failed runner for twenty-two years. The *Couch to 5K* training programme is more like *Couch to 0.5K* for me. But I still realise the importance of exercise and self-care, so I work out three times weekly (most weeks). Some climb mountains, run marathons and train for triathlons in pursuit of physical and mental health, while many others sweat in the gym or enhance their health through yoga, meditation or counselling.

We invest time, income and energy in our health because we understand the necessity of physical and mental well-being. So, I'm often baffled and frustrated that we devote too little focus to our financial well-being – a crucial cornerstone of our mental health.

As a nation, I don't think we've grasped the link between physical and mental health and financial well-being. Nor do we recognise that managing our finances is complementary to achieving overall wellness. I believe everyone should take steps to achieve financial wellness in the same way we exercise and eat a balanced diet for a healthy body.

Now, I don't expect my clients to track their net worth like they track their daily step count but, ideally, I'd like to see individuals take their financial well-being as seriously as their physical fitness.

Reading this book is a great start to actively managing your money and achieving better financial wellness. However, in financial matters, we sometimes need more help. When I have a headache, I know to take an aspirin, but if I suspect a brain haemorrhage, I don't attempt to cure it myself. Just as we sometimes consult doctors for our health, it's important to consult a financial professional when making big financial decisions. I'd encourage an annual or biennial check-up on our fiscal health with a finance professional.

What if I don't want to talk about money?

Believe me, you're not alone. I encounter a lot of resistance to talking about money. But if we can't talk about money, it's hard to work on improving our financial wellness. Some people will discuss the innermost details of their sex life with a therapist but can't disclose bank statements to a financial planner.

> ### CLIENT CASE
> ### PAVEL, AGED 42
> I can remember this client, even though I saw him quite a few years ago. Pavel first came to me for a pension consultation. I went into financial-planner mode and asked him about his debts, mortgage and

investments. His expression was a picture. He looked like I'd slapped him with a dead fish.

'What? Why would you ask me that?' he said. 'That's my private business and don't be trying to sell me any other shit. I'm here for a pension.'

Attempting to reassure him, I explained buying a pension might not be appropriate if he had a lot of short-term debt, for example. I don't think I convinced him. It's fair to say getting some clients to open up about their finances is challenging.

What about problem debt?

Getting people to talk can be even more challenging when they fall into serious financial difficulties. More than a third of people (35%) would find it hard to open up about their financial troubles, according to a Irish survey by iReach in 2022.

The head-in-the-sand approach is common, but money worries are nothing to be ashamed of. Remember, most people have no formal training or education in finances, even though it permeates every aspect of our lives. Fear of appearing ignorant or feelings of embarrassment and inadequacy can make a dangerous situation worse.

Isn't discussing money 'vulgar'?

In Ireland, we have far too many social inhibitions about discussing money. If someone in America buys a new car, it's normal for a friend to ask, 'How much did you pay for it?' If I asked that at a dinner party in Ireland, I'd never get invited back again.

Discussing money openly here is almost seen as some breach of societal etiquette. It's probably a hangover from British colonialism when refined aristocratic society deemed discussing money as crass and common. Wealth was never to be explicitly acknowledged or flaunted.

So, we grow up here believing money is a private concern and that discussing it is impolite, vulgar and brash. People who talk about their money 'have notions' or are 'show-offs'. Only in Ireland do you hear that deprecating reply: 'What? This old thing? Sure, I bought it in Penneys for a fiver.'

Let's make this clear: there's nothing shameful about talking about money. Financial well-being is not about filthy lucre, bling lifestyles, materialism or accumulating money for its own sake. It's about gaining control and feeling empowered about your spending habits. Our stress levels reduce when we achieve the freedom to pursue our passions and dreams. Managing our finances enables us to lead happier and healthier lives and have an improved quality of life.

What is financial well-being?

Financial well-being is the peace of mind and security we get from being in control of our money. Whether or not we like it, money is fundamental to our lives and can positively or negatively impact our general well-being and health.

Research shows that financial stability can positively affect us by reducing stress and giving us a sense of freedom and autonomy. If we struggle to pay for basics like food, shelter and healthcare, it's difficult to exhale. We feel trapped because we have no choices. The financial crisis from 2008 exacted an enormous physical and emotional toll on so many people. Anyone who experienced the cold face of a crash knows the importance of financial wellness. Like many, I witnessed people afflicted with stress-related illnesses and mental-health issues during the worst of those years.

Thankfully, we learned our lesson and are now a better, healthier nation. After a short, sharp shock, many worked hard to clear their debts. We began focusing on work–life balance and mental health rather than fast cars and apartments in Dubai.

The Consumer Financial Protection Bureau (CFPB) in the United States – the equivalent of our Central Bank of Ireland – has defined financial well-being to be:

- having control over day-to-day, month-to-month finances
- having the capacity to absorb a financial shock
- being on track to meet financial goals
- having the financial freedom to make the choices that allow you to enjoy life.

You'll note there are no mentions of words like 'pension', 'investment', 'mortgage', 'property' or 'tax'. Contrary to what some banks, financial planners and car sales agents may tell you, financial well-being is *not* linked to the products or services they want you to buy.

For me, the critical part of the statement is the final point – 'have the financial freedom to make the choices that allow you to enjoy life' – that part of the definition is the essence of financial well-being and good planning.

Let's break down this definition further.

What does 'control over finances' mean?

This boils down to being able to reach the weekly or monthly payday without running into financial difficulty.

You succeed if you get to payday without using an overdraft, missing a direct-debit payment, or borrowing from family and friends. You must have one euro (yes, that's all you need) in your account by payday.

One euro is not a comfortable financial situation, but it's significant. It means you can manage what's coming in and going out without running up debt or missing any payments. If this sounds like you, take a pat on the back. You're on the first step of the personal finance and financial well-being ladder.

Being good at finance doesn't entail a bank of screens on your desk tracking the S&P 500 or the Dow Jones. Step one is just being able to reach payday without being in trouble.

What does 'capacity to absorb a financial shock' mean?

A financial safety net is vital and is a subject close to my heart. In Section 5 (Financial Protection), I'll discuss the best options to protect your income, family and business in greater depth.

To increase our financial well-being, we need various reserves or financial products to cope with sudden economic shocks. Some believe financial shock refers to loss of income from a critical-illness diagnosis or redundancy. Financial shock for others is an appliance or a car breaking down. Section 1 (Personal Budgeting) will discuss the importance of a financial plan and having an emergency fund.

How do I know I'm 'on track to meet financial goals'?

Our financial goals are our objectives to reach in the short term or further down the road. It might mean clearing a bank loan or saving for a house – whatever the aim, it's easier to reach our goals if we identify them first.

My clients with clear goals and realistic timeframes are more likely to achieve them. They also enjoy the challenge of reaching those goals. As they say, it's the journey that counts, not the destination.

I always caution that some journeys are not worth the cost. I've witnessed many skewed efforts to be financially prudent. For example, I hear much about the Financial Independence Retire Early (FIRE) lifestyle movement. Followers advocate Spartan living with extreme saving and investing, so they are able to retire early. Many followers limit their social exchanges, miss family events and stress over every penny for decades. That's no way to live, and I'd never advise clients to meet financial goals this way.

Making smarter financial choices shouldn't mean postponing your life and happiness. We should still be able to enjoy life while engaging in sensible money management.

CLIENT CASE
JACK, AGED 40

It was clear from the minute Jack arrived in the office that he was feeling considerable stress. His tenancy was due to end in six months, and he pleaded for us to help him get approval for a mortgage.

Jack lived in a small two-bed apartment with his fiancée and two young children. At that time, he was working in a pharma company doing shift work. He was working early mornings, late nights and weekends to get money for a deposit.

First, we showed him government schemes he could use to help buy his own property. He wasn't aware that he was eligible for the schemes. So that gave him new options to consider and new hope.

But while doing a financial plan, we reviewed his pension plan. We discovered he had a phenomenal company plan. His employers were making a 10% employee contribution on top of his contributions. We showed him he was well on course to have a €750,000 fund when he reached his pension age.

I was stunned by Jack's reaction. He simply broke down in tears, and I'll never forget what he said: 'I thought I was failing my family.'

He was in such a fraught situation, but we showed the light at the end of the tunnel. His future looked bright. It wouldn't always be this stressful, and all his hard work was paying off. He left our offices feeling reassured and calmer, which is what financial planning should always do for people.

This is a common theme with clients who come in for a financial-planning consultation. People rarely understand their company pension scheme. Most don't know how much is being paid in or how it's invested.

From a financial planning perspective, it's impossible to plan for the future without understanding the details of your biggest future asset.

Do I need a lot of money to achieve financial well-being?

It all depends on your idea of financial well-being – the term means different things to people at various stages in their lives. For some, financial well-being is having a significant pension pot. For others, it is having savings for when the boiler breaks down. I meet people who find their financial well-being when we set up an eighteen-month plan to clear short-term loans or credit-card debt.

Today, my financial well-being is about spending time with my family and enjoying amazing travel experiences without counting every cent. Financial stability means a life where I can say *yes* more often.

Having the means to withstand a financial shock in day-to-day life provides you with a security net and an opportunity to breathe. It's a vital first step in financial well-being. If you can't move beyond day-to-day money struggles, debts are depriving you of planning for your life and that of your family in the future.

Of course, for some, financial well-being can also be about driving a Lamborghini or Ferrari. But I believe having the resources to survive some of life's curve balls is the biggest contributor to overall well-being.

How do I identify financial goals?

As each of us has a different idea of financial well-being, we all have our own reason or 'why' that may drive us to achieve it. Financial goals will vary according to your stage in life. The twenty-something singleton won't share the same big-picture objectives as someone decades older.

However, the first way to achieve our goals is to identify them. So, before going further, think about what financial well-being looks like for you.

Please grab a pen and list three goals that may help you achieve your financial well-being. Don't be afraid to think big. Consider what you want to achieve financially and the timeframe in which you'd like to achieve it.

If you're struggling to think of financial goals, below are the most common objectives cited by the clients I meet.

- To afford a house or save a deposit for one.
- To pay for house improvements.
- To pay for a car outright rather than getting a loan.
- To clear a mortgage or switch mortgage for a better rate.
- To save enough to start a business, leave a job or change careers.
- To afford early retirement.
- To establish an education fund for their children.
- To help older children get on the property ladder.
- To pass assets in a tax-efficient manner to their family.
- To afford maternity leave or unpaid leave.

- To buy a second property as an investment.
- To sell a business profitably.
- To travel the world.

What is the financial wheel?

If you ever attend a therapist, they may present you with a Wheel of Life in which you're asked to score aspects of your personal life. Sections of the wheel refer to our jobs, careers, relationships with partners, parents, etc. This therapy aid helps to identify areas in your life which need attention. If you score job satisfaction as number 1 but score your relationship as 4, it highlights a need to make a greater effort with your partner.

The revelations rarely surprise participants but, when they are highlighted, the wheel focuses the mind. People are more inclined to work on areas where they are failing when they see it presented to them in black and white.

This inspired me to devise a financial wheel that brings a similar focus to my clients and their path to financial well-being. Each of the seven sections combines to form a perfect circle of financial wellness to be addressed as you advance through life.

I've structured this wheel in order of relevance in our lives. The pension section, for example, comes sixth in the wheel, so it's dealt with after we've looked at budgeting, debt, protection, saving and investing. Your job is to identify which section of the wheel highlights your greatest concerns right now.

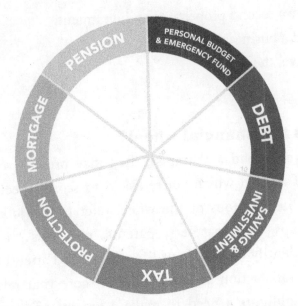

How do I use this book to increase my financial well-being?

The following seven sections of this book will reflect the seven sections of the financial wheel above.

Now, it's time to grab that pen again. This time, please score yourself from 1 to 7 according to your greatest concerns on the wheel.

- Do you worry most about clearing your debts? Then, Section 2 about Debt should score number 1 for you.
- Do you need to accumulate a financial safety net? Then, Section 1, Personal Budgeting, should be your go-to section.
- Do you fear that you'll never get on the mortgage ladder? Then, Section 6, Mortgages, will probably get your number 1.
- If you're twenty-five and living at home, you may look at Section 7, Pensions, and shrug your shoulders. This is not your priority, so score it as 6 or 7.

After awarding points to each section, I'd like you to read the following sections in the same order as your financial priorities. Your number-one priority or concern is the section to start with.

Of course, if you bought this book for general upskilling in personal finance, please go ahead and read the sectons in regular numeric order.

1	Personal Budgeting
2	Managing Your Debt
3	Saving and Investing
4	Tax
5	Financial Protection
6	Mortgages
7	Pensions

Will learning about financial well-being be difficult?

Not at all. We won't get bogged down in spreadsheets or the finer details of investment funds. We're not dealing with rocket science here. Personal finance is simple and logical. It doesn't take a genius to be good with money.

I called this book *Money Made Easy* because learning about financial well-being doesn't have to be complicated. At its heart, managing your personal finances is simple – *make more money than you spend or spend less than you earn.*

Of course, we all mess up with our finances, mainly because we lack knowledge and education in money-related matters.

Succumbing to impulse purchases is easy when consumer marketing has never been so pervasive. Many people overborrow or invest badly.

That's why we need financial planning. When our money is managed, it increases our quality of life, not our stress levels. We can all overcome our mistakes and turn our finances around if we learn to have a healthy relationship with money. I've seen it happen, and I've helped it happen time and time again.

If you have an income and the desire for change (and you clearly have if you are reading this), you can do it. A few simple steps now can lead to impressive payoffs in the long term. You can achieve financial well-being regardless of your starting point.

Who is this book for?

It's for everyone at all stages of life. Please remember that your path to financial well-being is unique to *your* life and circumstances. It is your needs and financial goals that are the priority.

When I explain why taking advantage of tax relief on pensions is the best way to build your future wealth, I don't mean to stress anyone without a pension. This book is not about adding stress to your life. Yes, there will be times when I'll discuss logical financial wins that everyone should, at some point, consider. However, even if the spreadsheet says something is a good idea, it doesn't mean it's a good fit for you right now.

I don't know you or understand what stage in life you are at. I don't know if you have an income of €27,000 or €97,000. If you're leaving college or about to retire. You may have a new mortgage and young children in a crèche.

Start by following the financial wheel and identifying *your* goals, and you're already on your way.

What will this book do for me?

My aim is to give you an understanding of where you are now financially, where you want to be and how to get there.

And I'd love this book to be passed through families and generations. Everyone should understand that sensible money management is not just a concept for the elite. Financial well-being is for all of us. And with some help and effort, we can turn our circumstances around.

Of course, achieving financial well-being is not an overnight process. Just as we dedicate ourselves to good physical and mental health, we must actively engage in our monetary wellness. By picking up this book, you've shown you're already on the path to making that positive difference in your life.

Only *you* can decide your goals and what you'd like your financial future to look like. The following sections will provide the tools and direction to help you put a comprehensive plan in place. My ultimate hope is that by following the *Money Made Easy* roadmap, you will secure your financial well-being and a better future for you and your family.

SECTION 1
PERSONAL BUDGETING

It's no accident that personal budgeting is the first section of the financial wheel. I place it first because it's the most critical part of a financial plan. Your personal budgeting plan is the foundation of success in managing your finances.

On the surface, managing finances should be easy – crunch some numbers, create a budget and stick to it. And, yes, it shouldn't take a genius to work out how to be good with money. After all, the first rule of thumb is simply to spend less than you earn. However, spending less than you earn seems challenging for many people. If it were easy, no one would end up with money problems.

Managing money is a skill and, like most skills, it requires a bit of effort and a little know-how. I hope the following section gives you the basics to enable you to become your own financial expert and significantly improve your life and finances.

What is budgeting?

I know some people shudder at the word 'budgeting'. For some, it conjures up thoughts of depriving themselves and being frugal. However, budgeting doesn't mean going on a money diet or swapping avocado and toast for beans on toast. (Although, you may need to cut back on the avocados if you're in a monthly deficit and unable to meet your bills.)

Good budgeting means balancing what comes into your account (income) and what goes out (expenses). It also means that if there's anything left over, you have a plan for the surplus.

At its core, budgeting is about financial planning and management. You may have heard the old saying, 'Look after the pennies and the pounds will look after themselves' – this sage advice means if you take care not to waste small amounts of money, you'll soon amass a large amount. And having more money means freedom, not frugality. To look after the pennies, you map out your income and expenses, identify where your money goes and where you can save more.

If you can't bear the phrase 'budgeting plan', just rename it your 'spending plan'. The truth is budgeting is less about restriction than making informed spending decisions. This is the route to greater financial freedom in the long term.

Why do we need to budget?

Setting sail without a compass is risky. Constructing a house without building plans is madness. Similarly, we need a budget plan to manage our money. A budget is a roadmap to greater financial health and well-being.

Without a budget, you're in greater danger of overspending, getting into debt or being unprepared for emergencies.

MY TOP TEN REASONS
WHY YOU MUST BUDGET

1. You gain control over your money and a sense of empowerment.

2. It keeps you focused on conscious spending. Practise this often enough and you will gain muscle memory, so it becomes second nature.

3. It gives you awareness of superfluous spending.

4. It helps you save when you couldn't before.

5. It helps you have more freedom to make better decisions as an individual, a couple or a family.

6. It identifies your weaknesses and where your income is disappearing to.

7. It frees up cash for more valuable and fulfilling parts of your life.

8. It makes you proactively consider loans, and negative or positive debt.

9. It improves relationships.

10. It guarantees better sleep, knowing you are financially secure.

Embrace budgeting as a part of your lifestyle. Life is hard enough, so do what you can to make it easier – a personal budgeting plan will make your life easier.

Who needs to budget?

Many people seem to think that budgeting is a task for people who are struggling financially on lower incomes. This is not the case. Everyone needs to have a budget, regardless of the size of their income or assets. Budgeting is beneficial whether you're a student, employee, retiree or business owner and whether you're on a large or small income. It's not about how much money you make, but how much you keep and grow.

Let's take the example of some of the highest-paid athletes in the world – National Football League (NFL) players in the United States.

Some players reportedly make over $100 million during their playing careers. Yet, they estimate an astonishing 78% of NFL players go bankrupt within two years of retirement. The reason for their bankruptcies? It's not about bad investment decisions. It's simply bad money management.

Why does money management go wrong?

There are many reasons people end up struggling with financial problems.

1. Unexpected expenses

Sometimes, we face difficulties because we have no safety net and are struck by unexpected expenses, such as medical emergencies, car breakdowns or even increased living costs. For example, few anticipated the rapid rise in domestic energy costs that happened in 2022. After the Russian invasion of Ukraine, soaring gas and electricity bills played havoc with household budgets across Europe.

2. Unreliable income

A fluctuating income also makes money management difficult. This is a problem faced by many working part-time, freelance or on contracts. However, it's even more important to budget and plan when your income is not steady or reliable. We can successfully navigate these speed bumps by adopting a flexible budgeting approach.

3. Bad money habits

From my experience, however, one of the main reasons money management goes wrong is bad money habits. Most people I see with money problems don't have an income issue – financial problems are rarely down to a lack of income – it's mostly down to how they spend the money. (Shopaholics, you know who you are.)

4. Borrowing too much

Probably the biggest reason for money problems is borrowing too much money. Debt lands many of us in trouble – no matter if it's credit cards, personal loans, car finance, etc.

It's important to realise there are two types of debt: good and bad. An example of good debt is a mortgage. Most of us will need a mortgage to buy a family home, which we pay back over time. Another example of good debt (if done correctly) is borrowing for an asset that produces surplus income to the monthly repayment – for example, buying an investment property and using the rental income to clear the mortgage.

Bad debt is short-term loans, such as credit cards, personal loans and car finance. Most financial planning experts encourage clients to avoid these debts because of the high interest rates. They advise clients to save money rather than borrow and pay interest for their purchases. I support that too.

I always say this: 'Your income should be used to grow your wealth. And when your money is tied up in repayments, you are making the banks and credit-card companies wealthy, not yourself. You are using your money to pay interest and make them rich.'

As soon as you sign a loan agreement, you're effectively signing over part of your income to a bank for months or years. I want my clients to own and have control over all their income. I want them to put their money to work for themselves. We do this best by saving for our needs rather than borrowing for them.

I will discuss this in more detail in Section 2 (Managing Your Debt). For now, I want to highlight that most budgeting issues come from too much debt repayment.

Why must I break bad money habits?

Your spending habits are directly correlated to your current financial situation. And if you're reading this section, I suspect you're unhappy with your current financial situation.

Many of us have worthy plans and goals, but we also have habits that scupper them. We might have a goal to lose ten pounds, but we have a habit of snacking on crisps at night. We might want to go to the gym before work, but we've got a habit of staying up too late watching endless episodes of our favourite series on Netflix.

When there's a gap between goals and daily habits, habits will always run roughshod over goals.

Similarly, a budgeting system is a plan or goal to meet financial targets, but you can't reach these goals if bad spending habits continue unchecked. And you are the only one who can change your spending habits. Nobody else.

A budgeting system is a plan to help you manage your income and expenses. You track both income and expenditure. Above all, you adjust your behaviours or spending habits to meet these financial goals.

How do I break a bad money habit?

Bestselling author James Clear discusses the four laws of behaviour change in his self-help book *Atomic Habits*. Many of Clear's teachings can apply to personal finance, and his first law of breaking a bad habit is to make it invisible.

For example, delete the Just Eat app from your phone if you spend too much on takeaway food. You simply remove all reminders of your bad habits from your environment. That way, you're not triggered when you see the app.

Are you spending too much on fashion online? Unsubscribe to those click-bait emails, updating you on new stock and special offers from your favourite fashion stores. Then, you are less likely to succumb to impulse purchases online.

Often, removing temptation is an excellent starting point for breaking bad money habits.

How do I start a good money habit?

My favourite budgeting tip for clients who struggle to save is also based on the make-it-invisible principle. I urge my clients to make their money invisible by setting up a direct debit to a savings account on payday. It's the path of least resistance. That way, my clients get to save the money before they have a chance to spend it.

Setting up a direct debit or standing order only takes a few minutes, and the regular saving habit is established. When the withdrawals are automated, you don't need to think about them again. A standing order is a regular payment that you can set up to transfer from your account to another account you own, other people's accounts or even to an organisation. You can amend or cancel the standing order from your side. A direct debit is when you authorise an organisation to debit money from your account. The direct debit can only be set up by this organisation and amended by them.

Whether the direct debit is €100 or €1,000 per month doesn't matter. It's a painless, automatic system that helps you achieve savings – and having savings is the start of good money management.

How do I join the fifty-two-week savings challenge?

Another of my efforts to get people to save is my fifty-two-week savings challenge, which I start up every January. It's designed to create a saving habit and build a nice pot of money. At the end of the year, you'll have an emergency fund or more savings to pay for things rather than borrowing from the bank or the credit union. The whole idea for the fifty-two-week challenge is to change money habits.

Many people get involved because it's easy to follow and stick with. We have two versions: the beginners and the advanced.

The beginner's challenge tasks you to save €1 in week one, €2 in week two, €3 in week three, and so on. By the final week, you're tasked to save €52, and your total savings will be €1,378.

If you want to kick your savings into high gear, take up the advanced challenge and start by saving €20 in week one, €35 in week two, €45 in week three, and €125 in week four. Follow the fluctuating pattern through and, by the final week, you're tasked to save the largest single amount in the challenge, which is €200, and you'll have saved €5,000.

You can also turn this challenge upside down and do it backwards if that works for you. You can download the challenge on www.askpaul.ie.

How does digital money hurt budgeting?

We all know the ways to spend money are numerous and proliferating. Convenience culture has its upsides and downsides for personal finances and budgeting. Once upon a time, we had to put on a coat and go to a shop or the local shopping centre to buy something. Now, we have the likes of Amazon and instant gratification. You see something, click on it, own it within minutes and have it delivered in days.

The problem is digital money makes spending far easier. Making purchases on your phone or with the simple tap of a card is effortless. When you don't have to peel out the notes from your wallet and physically hand over your hard-earned cash, the outgoings don't feel as real. We all have a greater tendency to frivolous spending when we can't see money in our purses or wallets physically dwindling.

Smartphones hold details of all our credit-card accounts, enabling us to pay for items painlessly and instantly. And 'tapping' money is now gone from a limit of €30 to €50 on our bank cards in Ireland. Spending is so easy that it leads to overspending. It's also harder to track our money when we're tap-tapping our way around town.

The rise of digital money has also led to a surge in subscription services, like streaming platforms or digital news outlets. Recurring payments to the likes of iTunes and Netflix can add up substantially over time.

What I am getting at here is that casual consumerism and the convenience culture hurt your budgeting – most overspending results from making a load of small purchases rather than one big one. To enhance your financial well-being, you must become more conscious of spending and actively change your money habits.

How to avoid the keeping-up-with-the-Joneses syndrome

Many of us engage with social-media platforms like Instagram, Facebook and TikTok where we're presented with constant updates showcasing people's fabulous lifestyles, possessions, experiences and achievements. We watch friends and influencers showcasing their glossy new kitchens or designer clothes and, if we're not careful, we can be sucked into budgeting problems with the 'bandwagon effect'. The bandwagon effect is a tendency for people to adopt certain behaviours or attitudes simply because others are.

We see posts that feature 'unboxings' or expensive gadgets, which can trigger feelings of inadequacy, fear of missing out and the urge to 'keep up'.

'Sure, everybody was using credit cards and buying what they wanted, and I did the same.' I heard this a lot after the economic crash in 2008. When your friends are getting new kitchens or cars, it's easy to persuade yourself you need one too.

Trying to emulate the lifestyles of others results in excessive spending beyond your means and financial stress.

First, please remember that most of what we're looking at is a mirage anyway. Social media only presents the 'Instagrammable' view of people's lives. It's important to remember that these 'perfect' images don't necessarily portray anyone's reality.

We've all heard the disparaging old Irish saying, 'They're all fur coats and no knickers'. This rather cruel remark is often directed at people who are outwardly bling and lavish, but who live on credit cards and loans. It might be an old saying, but it's often the perfect description for much of what we see on social media. Some people you know may look like they're living the designer lifestyle, but often it's on borrowed money. Let's face it: no one will tell you on TikTok about the sleepless nights when they ran up terrible credit-card debts.

Enjoy social media for what it is – a little information and a lot of fantasy and entertainment. Our focus shouldn't be on how others live their lives but on our own personal growth, achieving personal goals, and ultimately living a fulfilling life within our means.

Place value on experiences rather than possessions and stand firm with your budgets. Try a social-media detox or limit your time on Instagram if you find it's influencing you and making you spend more. Above all, be alert to the dreaded keeping-up-with-the-Joneses mindset and spend consciously.

Why is my budget system not working?

Some of you reading this section may be proactive about money management and feel that you are good at budgeting. Yet, you still feel your finances are tight and your budget is under pressure. That's not surprising, and if you're properly tracking your spending, you'll know it's because of inflation and the rise in consumer costs.

We discuss inflation and beating it in depth in Section 3 (Saving and Investing). Inflation is like an invisible tax that creeps up and robs you of your spending power. The inflation rate was over 8% in Ireland in 2022, meaning prices of everyday goods rose on average by that amount.

The price in supermarkets rose even more. Last year's weekly shopping budget of €150 has probably crept up to €200 a week. If your income hasn't risen by €50 a week, you are forced to adjust and find it elsewhere in your budget. A personal budgeting plan is not something that can be written in stone. Circumstances change, prices rise, income fluctuates, and emergencies happen.

How to run the family with a business mindset

My job is to trigger a shift in my clients' financial mindset – and for some of my clients, it helps them to think and act like they are running a family business.

Quiz

1. When your income exceeds your expenses, are you exempt from budgeting?
2. Is a budget a one-time financial plan?
3. Can budgeting help to reduce financial stress?
4. Does budgeting involve tracking your spending, or both your income and spending?

Answers: 1. No, 2. No, 3. Yes, 4. Both

CLIENT CASE
MARGARET & SHANE, AGED 45

The couple, both solicitors and earning substantial six-figure salaries, came to me in late 2022. They were running out of money by the end of every month. How do two people earning €20,000 a month or more run out of money? Because being good with money is unrelated to your profession or income. It's nothing to do with intelligence. It's a behaviour that all of us can learn, but few of us have innately.

The couple had requested to meet me about retirement planning, but I had to widen the conversation to their spending behaviour. There was absolutely no point continuing the pension-planning conversation. They would have required a massive pension to keep up with their spending habits. We had to start at the beginning and devise a personal budget for them.

CLIENT CASE
CAROL, AGED 26

Carol came to us a few years ago. At that time, she was a single mother of a one-year-old child and had lost her job, so her only income was from social-welfare benefits. Yet, she came to us to put her children's allowance into an investment account for her child's education.

I'm sure she could have used that children's allowance for many things, but she was adamant she could manage without it. She wanted to put it away every month for the next seventeen years to pay for college expenses. With an average return of 8%, she will have approximately €40,000 in her fund after taxes and charges when the child is ready to go to college.

I see people with huge salaries frittering away their money every month. So, I greatly admire people like Carol, who are so disciplined even though they live on the breadline. Despite her difficult circumstances, she looked to the future and prioritised her child's education. She turned a challenging situation into a positive achievement with clever planning and budgeting.

This isn't too far from the truth, personal budgeting is really similar to running a business.

Let's take the example of Mary and John, who have two children. The couple are like the joint managing directors of their own business, the most powerful positions in any organisation.

Their business is the family, and Mary and John's income is the company's turnover (or revenue). Generally, sales (their incomes) are steady. They may increase or decrease because of overtime, bonuses, etc. However, most clients I meet have predictable incomes, which is great for planning. Boring is often good.

The fixed expenses of your household are like the fixed overheads in a business. Substitute children for staff and property tax for rates, etc. Most businesses hire an independent accountant who helps manage the company's budgeting, finances and tax returns. Others have their own financial controller.

However, Mary and John must take on the dual role of managing directors and financial controllers. They must monitor the income and outgoings of their family business. They have to ensure they're making a profit. If a business struggles to make a profit, there are two choices – increase income or decrease expenses. Often, it's necessary to do both. It's the same when running the finances of a family.

How do I budget for a family?

The moment you have your first child, you realise your needs are now a distant second to your child's. That's okay, it's how it's supposed to be. With that, two things happen:
- You have new outgoings – such as baby food, crèche fees, weekly runs to the pharmacy, etc.
- You stop or reduce spending on yourself.

As a father of four children, I know kids are like a bonfire for your disposable income. I'm not even talking about the cost of third-level education yet. Suddenly, the fixed costs of running your family business rise dramatically. How do you adjust?

Being a parent involves becoming far more savvy with your cash, removing unessential luxuries and, above all, planning.

What are the five key steps in a family budget?

1. List all sources of monthly income

Our income is our most crucial wealth-building tool, but how often do you ever truly consider what you earn? It sounds so basic, but you'd be surprised. Most of us see our salary land in our account at the end of each month and don't consider it beyond that. I ask clients to list their household income, and they often forget about child benefit and bonuses.

It's impossible to budget without having full oversight of our monthly finances. Being in the dark about our finances also breeds anxiety and creates uncertainty.

Instead of muddling through, let's examine our earnings and learn the following.

- When is it coming in?
- What must be paid out when it lands?
- What will be left when that flurry of direct debits is paid?

If you can get a clear oversight of your income and outgoings, you will end up in a far sounder place, mentally and financially.

When you start budgeting, you often find that you fall into one of two brackets:

- You barely make ends meet because of the financial limitations of your salary/income.
  OR
- You have a good salary, but things are tight and not as promising as your income would suggest. This is the more frustrating bracket, but it's the easier one to fix. You have a good earning capacity but are not good with your money.

2. List all the monthly outgoings

We have a lot of expenditure to identify.

- List the costs of the essentials, such as mortgage or rent, childcare and your average spend on utilities.
- Add the costs of the kids' football club or dance group. Costs associated with health and social skills are non-negotiable. Don't forget the cost of the gym, playing five-a-side, dance classes or whatever you do for your health and fitness.
- Add the variable expenses such as the weekly shopping. Don't lowball these figures. If grocery shopping varies between €150 to €200 a week, then budget for €200. It's a win if you have a surplus at the end of the week.
- What about medical costs? How much, on average, do you spend in the chemist or at the doctor?
- What are your fuel costs?
- What other extracurricular activities are there? Include them if they're a part of your family life.
- Add up all your annual costs – property tax, motor tax, TV licence, house insurance and car insurance – and divide by twelve to get your monthly expenditure. For example: property

tax €600, motor tax €390 + TV licence €160 = €1,150 annually – which averages at €95 per month.

- Don't forget those death-by-a-thousand-cuts costs that you tap away each week. Are you buying lunch several times a week at work? That's easily €30 a week, €120 a month or €1,440 a year (which amounts to €2,000-plus of salary depending on your tax band).
- What other social, personal and well-being costs do you have? Are they fixed or variable? For example, a clothes budget, a date-night budget or a night at the cinema. Remember the Netflix account, iTunes and Amazon Prime. Check your credit-card spending – where is it going? Some of these costs are important and reasonable. Family budgeting is not a constant cycle of self-punishment.

Like any business with margins and running costs, the more honed and accurate a picture you have of your budget, the better your business performs.

3. Work out ways to reduce outgoings

Identifying your income and outgoings lets you examine your ways to reduce outgoings. Do you really need Netflix, Disney+ and Amazon Prime? If you subscribe monthly, you could spend up to €435 a year. They seem like small monthly costs, but subscriptions add up. They're part of the death of your budget by a thousand cuts.

Do you change your gas and electricity providers every year? That's a guaranteed win for very little effort. Can you get a better rate on your mortgage? Can you cut out one takeaway a month?

Can you encourage the family to walk or cycle more and save on fuel?

When you have identified your expenditure, you're in a better position to see where savings can be made.

4. Plan and save for large purchases, holidays and future goals

When you have children, you must look beyond next month and plan for the long term.

By itemising your income and spending, you can free up cash for more long-term planning. Let's take, for example, Mary and John, who have two young children. They have cut their monthly budget and just saved €150 – which they can now use elsewhere. Mary and John decide to use these savings to take the pressure off themselves in eighteen years by using them to fund a third-level college fund for the kids.

Investing €150 a month for eighteen years should yield a return of more than €40,000 by the time the children are ready for college. That extra €150 a month helps Mary and John achieve a long-term goal.

5. Avoid credit cards and short-term debt

Achieving stage four of the key steps in a family budget means that you can achieve number five. The cornerstone of sound financial planning is steering clear of short-term loans. You can avoid the debt trap when you make savings in your budget and have a surplus.

Mary and John could have also used that surplus of €150 a month to upgrade their car in three years' time. This would save them a fortune in interest payments if they needed to take out a loan for the car.

Think about your purchases. Christmas and first communions are scheduled events, so plan for them. Put off buying the car until you have a much larger deposit for a new one. Save for that holiday instead of putting it on the credit card. If you cannot afford it now, wait. Whatever your heart desires will still be there when you save the money – and you'll enjoy it more when you don't have the stress of debt.

How do I budget as a single person?

I am blessed as I was raised in a two-parent family. I've also raised my children as part of a couple. If you're a single parent on a single income source, you can probably write this section better than I can.

When I talk about single, I'm referring to a single-earning household. You may or may not be in a relationship. You may live alone or with children – by single, I mean you are an adult paddling your own canoe in terms of making an income.

Budgeting as a single person has its upsides and downsides. If you're single, your budget may be affected in several ways:

- You face more significant risks because you bear all the financial responsibilities, unlike a couple who can share expenses.
- You don't have the safety net of a household with a second income. This can become significant during a job loss or other unexpected financial emergencies.
- You lose out on economies of scale that couples enjoy. The

electricity bill doesn't double for a couple. A single person can pay as much as any couple for gas, electricity, rent, vehicle costs and insurance without the ability to split the costs.

- Saving for a deposit for a mortgage on your own is a slog. Anyone who does it has my utmost admiration. It takes double the time without a partner contributing, and your ability as a single earner to borrow is much reduced.
- The tax system is also less favourable to single people with no children. The single earner is often overlooked, as government budgets focus on the family unit.
- Your financial goals may differ. If you're single and childless, you don't consider school fees or a larger family home but can prioritise travel or retirement savings.
- If you're single, you have greater control over your disposable income when you don't have to factor in a partner's needs. Therefore, if you're single with no children, your budget might have more room for personal hobbies, entertainment or travel.

How do I reduce the risks of personal budgeting as a single person?

Your budget needs to be more agile and more streamlined when you rely on a single source of income. The five key steps in forming a family budget outlined above apply to you too, but with greater urgency. The single person needs to be intentional with spending.

- Create a budget – see steps 1, 2 and 3 of the five key steps in a family budget. Track your income and expenses to understand where your money goes.

- Identify necessary expenses and areas where you can cut back. The handbrake should be on when it comes to spending. The single earner must clearly differentiate between wants and needs.
- Save and invest wisely. Aim to save and invest a percentage of your income monthly.
- Have an emergency fund. It should be enough to cover your living expenses for three to six months. This will protect you in case of job loss or sudden expenses.
- Enhance your career prospects by gaining extra qualifications and taking on additional responsibilities. I realise it is more difficult for single parents to look for opportunities to earn extra money.
- Consider having multiple streams of income as a form of income insurance. This could include working a second job, freelance work or starting a side business.
- If you are single without children and have the space, consider getting a roommate to share rent and utility expenses.
- Take out critical illness cover or income protection that will cover your lost income in the event of an accident or illness.
- Eliminate short-term debts and avoid unnecessary credit-card spending. You have nowhere to hide and no one to help you if something happens and you can no longer pay those debts.
- Use any surplus to plan for retirement and start your retirement plan as soon as you can. If you remain single until retirement, surviving alone on the state pension will be difficult.

CLIENT CASE
PAUL, AGED 30

Paul had no children or mortgage. He was good at what he did, but his career was drifting and he was given the opportunity to become involved in a start-up.

He was naturally conservative, and the safe option was to stay employed and progressing up the career and income ladder. But, on the other hand, he also had no responsibilities. He took the chance on the start-up. He had a few rocky years initially and experienced times when he felt he made a mistake. However, the business bore fruit after three years.

He took the risks when he could and increased his earning power. There are advantages as well as risks to being a single earner. If Paul had a mortgage or children, etc., it's unlikely he would have taken the chance. Your freedom as a single-income person means you have more control over your destiny. Use it well.

How do I budget in a relationship?

Disagreements over money are one of the most common conflicts between couples. Rows can erupt over different spending habits, incomes, debts or lack of clear communication about financial expectations and goals. Financial disagreements are one of the main causes of marriage breakdown (after infidelity).

However, most of this conflict can be avoided by having open, honest and regular discussions about finances, planning and budgeting together – and by respecting each other's money habits and needs.

Nevertheless, budgeting within a relationship may raise specific concerns.

- Do you have joint or separate accounts – or both? Each option has pros and cons, so deciding what suits you both is essential.
- You need to communicate openly about money. Discuss your financial worries, expectations and priorities with each other. Create a budget that works for both of you.
- Transparency is key. There should be no secrets when it comes to finances in a relationship.
- Create a budget – see steps 1, 2 and 3 of the five key steps in a family budget. Start by listing all the sources of income you have as a couple, individually or jointly. When you clearly know your income, next list all your expenses. When you have set your budget, start tracking and monitoring your costs.
- Work out a plan to share the bills. If you're both on a similar income, paying 50/50 is ideal. However, if there are considerable discrepancies in your earnings, this can lead to rows or resentment. The word is 'compromise' – work out something between you that is fair and clear.
- Make paying bills transparent and trackable. When your income and outgoings are established, consider setting up a joint or new account for all bills. If one person pays by direct debit and another contributes from Revolut, tracking who's paying what is a nightmare.

- Make a plan for paying off debts like car loans, credit cards or other loans. Ignoring this can cause additional stress in the relationship.
- Are you picturing the life you want to live together and making joint goals? Maybe it's buying a house, travelling or starting a family. Agree on a plan and how you'll save for it.
- People have different spending habits; one might be a saver while the other is a spender. But that does not mean it cannot work. You need to find common ground and stick to your budget.
- Set realistic goals that both of you can follow. Otherwise, you are setting yourselves up for failure, conflict and blame.
- Make sure you both have your own disposable income for incidentals and nights out with separate friend groups. Ring-fence a portion of your own pay for discretionary spending.

I understand that starting the money conversation with a partner or spouse is difficult if you have never done this before. But couples find plenty to fight about – don't add money to the rows.

Open the conversation by having a mini-money challenge based on goals. Each person writes down three financial goals – one short, medium and long term. Then, you swap the goals and discuss each one. Hopefully, some or all three are aligned. However, if they're not, that's not necessarily a bad thing. You are learning now and can start a conversation about your priorities and goals.

Hopefully, after reading *Money Made Easy*, you can then work on a plan to achieve all of your goals.

Why we don't get hung up on spreadsheets and systems

We can use many spreadsheets and budgeting systems for our budgeting plan. And, yes, spreadsheets can be helpful tools for organising and analysing financial data. However, the problem with number-crunching systems is that they exclude the emotional and behavioural factors that influence financial decisions. Spreadsheets don't understand impulsive spending or emotional triggers, they focus on numbers and calculations, which can feel detached from real life.

As a result, I'm not a huge fan of spreadsheets and the various models of budgeting systems out there. Every day, I see that personal budgeting involves factors beyond mere numbers. Spending habits also affect human behaviour and psychology. Ignoring these factors creates a mediocre budget plan that's not relatable nor inspirational for most of us.

Also, a plan may make perfect sense when you make it, but no plan remains static. Like everything, it must move with the times and the changing environment. Spreadsheets may be able to compute precise number manipulations, but their straight boxes, rows and columns do not always adapt to the erratic scenarios in real life.

I don't want to see you pour all your efforts into rows and columns of numbers. My intention is for you to undergo a shift in your approach to how you understand and perceive money.

What does a new 'mindset' in money management mean?

- Recognising that money is a tool that can support your goals and desires.
- Educating yourself on topics like budgeting, saving and investing.
- Learning mindful money management. I want you to think about the whys behind your financial choices rather than solely focusing on the how much.
- Differentiating between needs and wants, practising financial discipline and making conscious financial decisions.
- Setting clear and realistic goals and having a proper roadmap. I want you to save some of your income, pay off debt and invest in your future.
- Switching your mindset from 'I wish I could afford this' to 'I could afford this, but I choose to spend on other priorities'.

What are personal budgeting models?

There are various personal budgeting models that you can follow that I will highlight below. I don't particularly like any of them because, as I've said above, I find many too rigid. But if you see something among them that works for you, great.

Remember, ultimately, no one and no system can help improve your finances – only you can make that change.

Set your financial goals, list your income, record your expenditure and see if you can reduce any of your outgoings. Set a limit for disposable income. Then, consciously decide how to allocate any surplus to achieve your financial goals.

Remember that budgeting models aren't one-size-fits-all. What works for one person might not work for another. So, choose a strategy that aligns best with your financial situation and goals, or be creative and set up a hybrid of systems that work for you. You can find many apps that help you to track your spending. The askpaul.ie website also has a dynamic budgeting tool you can download for free to help measure your income and outgoings.

There are also many suggestions for budgeting models online, including the following.

The envelope system

We used the envelope system all the time in askpaul years ago, but since people stopped using cash, it became less relevant. The envelope system is a cash-based budgeting system. You allocate your cash for different spending categories into separate envelopes. When the money in an envelope is gone, spending is finished in that category. It was an effective system to avoid overspending, but it's more difficult to use now in the era of Revolut and digital transactions.

I still think if you're struggling with budgeting, you need to go to the ATM, take cash out and only use cash where possible. Otherwise, it's too easy to tap dance around town with your debit card. Too many people are just going, tap, tap, tap, tap, and end up clueless about where their money has gone.

The reverse budget

This is also known as the 'pay yourself first' method. It's a version of my 'make your money disappear' method of saving. With this system, saving and investing are prioritised. When your wages land in your account, a percentage of your money is whipped away by direct debit for savings and investments or retirement. Only then can you start spending, and the remaining income is divided among your expenses.

Using it as a system, however, doesn't always work. Because there's less emphasis on tracking your spending, you risk overspending. Then, you end up dipping into your savings anyway to make it to the end of the month.

The values-based budget

This is about allocating money towards what matters most to you first, whether that's travel or paying off debt. You spend your money in a way that aligns with your values. You start by deciding your spending and saving priorities and then build a specific financial plan around them. You spend your money based on what provides you maximum happiness or value in life, while you spend less on areas that mean little to you.

This is great if you decide that spending time with others makes you happiest or if buying your first home makes your heart beat a little faster. But it's not so great if what makes you happiest is champagne-filled club nights or buying expensive gadgets.

Zero-based budgeting

This is a business model that's sometimes adapted for personal budgeting. The basic idea is that your income minus your expenses equals zero at the end of the month. So, if your take-home pay is €2,800 a month, then everything you save or spend should add up to €2,800. Every euro has to be accounted for and has a job or goal. This system promotes intentional spending but requires a lot of planning and tracking. It's very time-consuming, so I don't see it working over the long term for many. For me, the time cost is too high.

The 50/30/20 rule

This suits some people. It's simple, flexible and suitable for beginners. It mainly involves setting up direct debits and tracking what you spend the rest of the time.

This system divides your take-home pay into three categories:
- 50% is allocated to needs and core essentials, such as rent, mortgage, childcare and food and whatever else is part of your core essentials.
- 30% is allocated for wants, like Sky Sports, handbags, evenings out, weekend breaks, holidays and funding hobbies.
- 20% is allocated towards savings, investments and debt repayment.

In an ideal world, the 50/30/20 would work. However, I don't find it very useful because everyone is so different regarding their personal finances. I've completed thousands of financial plans for clients and met people who spend 80% of their income on core essentials. Most of their money goes into keeping a roof over their head, food on the table, the lights on and clothes on their back. The 50/30/20 rule, in this case, is simply not going to work.

The advantages of this system are that it focuses your mind and makes you think about how you prioritise your spending. And I like any plan that emphasises the clearing of loans. I always encourage clients to rid themselves of short-term debt. If you can shed that credit card debt costing €250 a month, it can be put into savings and investments. Having a small nest egg and no short-term debts can also be priceless in terms of peace of mind.

TOP TEN WAYS TO IMPROVE YOUR BUDGETING

1. Stick to a grocery list to avoid impulsive purchases.
2. Use energy-saving appliances and switch supplier every year to cut utility bills.
3. Practise mindful spending.
4. Create an emergency fund.
5. Pay off debts as swiftly as possible.
6. Continually reassess your budget.
7. Set realistic financial goals.
8. Adjust discretionary spending and review subscriptions.
9. Invest wisely to grow your income.
10. Use an app or spreadsheet to make tracking your budget more manageable.

CLIENT CASE
PETER & SARAH, AGED 35 & 34

Peter and Sarah are new clients with two children who came to me in early 2023.

They filled out their information on the digital fact-finding form that I send clients before I meet them. (See the budgeting template on pp70–2.) It's a comprehensive form that gets clients thinking and helps inform me about their financial situation.

On paper, everything seemed fine. They looked in good shape, with a combined income of salaries and child benefits amounting to a healthy €8,880 monthly. They were five years into their mortgage.

Why did they need me, and why were they flustered when they arrived?

We could all see on the forms they completed that 30% of their income was not accounted for at the end of the month. The documents weren't painting the complete picture. They admitted they were struggling, even though their forms indicated they should have had €2,620 left in their accounts every month.

When I dug a little deeper, the rosy picture crumbled.

They didn't pool their expenditure and didn't include personal spending from their separate accounts. They were not saving much at all. All they put aside for emergencies was €250 a month, which amounted to less than 3% of their income.

One person had a smaller income of €2,500 per month. But this was an average figure, as the person was a part-time, self-employed sole trader. They had no disciplined system for spending and no ring-fenced allocations for bills. They were completely reactionary in all spending, scrambling to meet the next bill.

Their 'lifestyle' spend was high, money was running through their fingers, and they had nothing to show for it.

I didn't even broach switching their mortgage. I never mentioned financial products or pensions, even though they needed to start saving. Instead, we agreed they would return in six months after a financial reset. They would change how they treated money as a couple. They were no longer two separate financial entities with two different agendas. They were a family business and needed to control their income and expenditure, or they were in danger of failing as a business. They required an entirely new way of thinking about money.

Family budgeting does not require a PhD, but it does need joined-up thinking and transparency.

When Peter and Sarah returned, they had turned their family business around. They knew their income and all their outgoings. After reining in their spending, they realised they had €2,500 a month surplus rather than the fictional €2,620 that appeared on the forms they provided.

With that, we moved into action:

- We saved the couple even more money by changing protection and mortgage products.
- We arranged retirement savings for them both.
- We set up a college fund for the kids.
- We initiated a plan to build up a short-term, six-month reserve of savings.

Peter and Sarah are starting 2024 in a completely different space from where they were at the beginning of 2023.

INCOME	€8,880.00
Particulars	**Actual (€)**
Income Source 1	6,100.00
Income Source 2	280.00
Income Source 3	2,500.00

EXPENSES	€6,010.00
Particulars	**Actual (€)**
Rent/Mortgage	1,415.00
Electricity	350.00
Gas	00.00
Mobile phone	120.00
Broadband	130.00
Home insurance	35.00
TV packages	00.00

TV licence	15.00
Childcare	1,000.00
Car loan	00.00
Petrol/Diesel	350.00
Car insurance	75.00
Groceries	1,200.00
Personal care (salon/barber)	50.00
Transport (parking/bus/Luas)	00.00
Health insurance	00.00
Life assurance	220.00
Other insurance	00.00
Personal loan	00.00
Credit union loan	00.00
Credit card 1	00.00
Credit card 2	00.00
Club membership (gym, golf, etc.)	60.00
Pets (food, vet, etc.)	00.00
Clothing/Shoes	200.00
Gifts	00.00
Entertainment (nights out, cinema, meals)	200.00
Online shopping	50.00
Online subscriptions	40.00
Other	500.00

SAVINGS	€250.00

Particulars	Actual (€)
Credit union	250.00
Deposit	00.00
Educational fund	00.00

Pension	00.00
One-off fund (home/car repairs, etc.)	00.00
Annual fund (holidays, Christmas, etc.)	00.00
Back to school	00.00
Life insurance	00.00
Emergency fund	00.00

The final word on personal budgeting

Like learning any new skill, budgeting requires practice and determination. However, when you master it, you'll realise budgeting is not about rationing pennies but about achieving your financial freedom.

Ultimately, budgeting is about using your income and money to serve your goals and dreams. I hope the information in this section will help you embark on a new relationship with money and start making conscious financial decisions for your life.

Your 7-point action plan for personal budgeting

- Identify your income and expenses.
- Set realistic financial goals.
- Categorise your expenses.
- Track your spending.
- Adjust your budget according to lifestyle changes.
- Cultivate the habit of saving.
- Regularly review and modify your budget.

SECTION 2
MANAGING YOUR DEBT

What is debt?

Debt is spending money today that you hope to earn in the future. It's a form of borrowing from your future self.

Debt is a normal part of life. We're out for lunch with friends and are short on cash. A pal lends us a tenner – we're in debt to that friend until we pay back that €10. Now expand that lunch loan to bigger things, like getting a car loan. We go to a bank or a credit union for larger loans and sign a legal contract to repay an amount with an agreed interest rate at a future date.

This interest is a 'thank you' to the lender for the privilege of using their money. The thank you can also be very expensive, depending on the type of debt you take out. For example, credit-card debt can range from 14–23% per year. A personal loan would typically range from 6–9%.

Why do I need to learn about debt?

Debt is a tool and when we use most tools, we need to read the safety instructions first. By the end of this section, I hope you recognise debt as a tool to be used with caution, like a powerful chainsaw.

Used correctly, debt can open doors and lead to greater freedom and a better quality of life. However, like any tool, improper use of debt can be dangerous. Problem debt is not just a financial issue, jeopardising your living standards and prospects; when not managed properly, debt can have a corrosive effect on your physical and mental health and your relationships with those close to you.

We're going to learn to understand debt better so we know how to control it and how to use it, so that it adds enhancement rather than distress to our lives.

Why do we have debt?

Debt enables us to have some financial flexibility. Sometimes, we have needs we can't afford straightaway, so we borrow money from our future earnings to meet those needs. For example, we all need shelter but rarely can anyone afford to buy a house outright. So, we borrow money from a bank and have mortgage debt for twenty or thirty years. Debt is a financial facility with many advantages for those who use it properly.

Who has debt?

Anyone who spends more money than they have available to them has debts. If you use credit cards for day-to-day purchases, you have debt. Many of us have debts for large expenses, such as a home or car. Even governments borrow money to fund expenditures like roads, schools, hospitals and other infrastructure projects. They do this through government bonds and 'state savings' accounts sold by An Post and the National Treasury Management Agency (NTMA).

Most of us have some sort of debt as it helps us to fund items we can't afford now and helps us to manage our cash flow.

What is good debt?

Debt isn't inherently bad. Responsible borrowing helps you achieve important goals, like owning a home or furthering your education.

Good debt is used to fund something that is considered an investment. Buying a home or a second property with a rental opportunity may be investments worth borrowing for. Debt can fund master's and other postgraduate courses. Any borrowings that increase long-term income are good debts.

Good debts serve a real purpose and fund needs rather than wants. Taking on debt of this kind makes sense.

What is bad debt?

The key to managing debt lies in differentiating between good debt and bad debt. The latter doesn't serve a purpose and can lead to financial hardship and stress. Often, bad debt results from wants rather than needs. 'Needs' and 'wants' are fundamental concepts in personal finance and are closely tied to debt. Needs are basic living requirements and include housing, medical care, food and transport.

You may want a top-of-the-range Tesla or BMW but don't need it. Similarly, you may want an expensive gadget, a brand-new kitchen and a set of new golf clubs. While fulfilling these desires and buying those golf clubs can enhance your lifestyle, you should pay for them with savings or disposable income – however, many people fall into the trap of using debt to make this type of purchase instead.

Debt becomes a problem if it is used too often to cover your wants rather than needs. When people regularly borrow money to afford their lifestyle, they can end up with problem debt.

What kind of debtor are you?

From my daily interactions with clients, I've come across three types of borrower.

- The cool borrowers These people understand and feel comfortable with debt, with little anxiety. They view debt as a tool to achieve specific goals and are confident about their ability to repay their debt. This approach can still lead to problems if their circumstances change.
- The overwhelmed borrowers These are people who fear debt to the point that it overwhelms them. Sometimes, they are

people who struggle to control their spending behaviours and, sometimes, their stress arises from unexpected emergencies or large amounts of debt accumulated over time. Either way, they cannot keep up with their payments for multiple debts and feel trapped by their current situation.

- **The ignorant borrowers** These people wear blinkers despite their growing debts. This can be due to denial or fear – though, sometimes, it's because they struggle to control their spending and lack understanding about their finances. For whatever reasons, they ignore the problem, and this avoidance leads to missed payments, mounting debts and serious financial consequences. They end up in danger of losing their homes and even bankruptcy. Debtors who are in denial are the hardest to deal with because they don't recognise the problem or wrongly believe their debt issues can be resolved magically.

What is financial distress?

I want to add a caveat to this section on debt: financial distress is different to problem debt. If you cannot meet the cost of living and are struggling to pay for rent, food and utility bills, this is an emergency. Your problems are beyond the scope of this book at the moment.

If you've taken out a loan to pay off another debt, you are in survival mode – and you may need immediate intervention and support.

Help is available for those in severe financial distress.

- **The St Vincent de Paul** offers practical help to people through its nationwide services. They help with money issues if you contact the office in your area.

- The Department of Social Protection has a scheme called the Supplementary Welfare Allowance (SWA), which may be helpful. The scheme helps pay for a big utility bill or the costs of a one-off item. Two payment types under the scheme may apply: the Exceptional Needs Payment and the Urgent Needs Payment.
- If you are behind on mortgage payments, there are specific steps and protections for you. The process for mortgage arrears is detailed on the Money Advice and Budgeting Service (MABS) website (mabs.ie). MABS is a free Irish money-advice service. It helps people in serious mortgage arrears as part of the Abhaile scheme and the Dedicated Mortgage Arrears (DMA) service.
- Those with a low income, few assets and debts of less than €35,000 can avail of a Debt Relief Notice (DRN) for money problems. You need to contact MABS for advice, though this scheme doesn't apply to mortgage holders.
- Another form of debt settlement is a Debt Settlement Arrangement (DSA), which focuses on overdrafts, personal loans and credit cards.
- A DSA can help write off some parts of a debt. A Personal Insolvency Practitioner (PIP) helps you to handle the DSA process. PIPs are accountants, solicitors or barristers who train in personal insolvency and mortgage arrears. You can search for a PIP in your area or contact MABS to arrange the service.
- The last option for some is bankruptcy, which requires professional advice beyond the scope of this book. For this to be an option, you must have debt above €20,000. Bankruptcy lasts a year, with an agreed debt written off under an arrangement. Again, a PIP is required here.

WHAT IS PROBLEM DEBT?

When you owe money and cannot keep up with the repayments, your debt has become a problem. Problem debt can have severe consequences, like legal action from lenders and personal stress. It often occurs because of changes to someone's financial circumstances, such as job loss or unforeseen emergencies. But, sometimes, it's due to overspending, inadequate budgeting or lack of financial literacy.

Signs of problem debt

Are you:

- Struggling to keep up with bill payments and missing direct debits?
- Only able to make minimum payments on your credit cards?
- Borrowing money from people to pay bills and catch up with arrears?
- Attempting to open new credit cards in order to pay off old cards or other debts?
- Using credit cards for necessities like food or rent?
- Receiving letters and calls from creditors and debt collectors?
- Consistently overdrawn at the bank?
- Constantly worried or stressed about how you'll make your next payment?
- Afraid of answering the phone or opening post due to creditor calls or letters?

How do I avoid or reduce unnecessary debt?

You've heard the cliché: 'If you fail to plan, you plan to fail.' These phrases become clichés because they hold more than a kernel of truth. They're often based on observations and everyday experiences. And if you want to clear bad debt, you need to make a plan.

There's also truth in the cliche: 'Insanity is doing the same thing over and over and expecting different results.' Fretting about debt but continuing to spend makes a bad situation worse. Stop the handwringing and start tackling it.

If you want your financial situation to change, you must change your own behaviour. You need to stop and consider every purchase. Mindful spending and a good savings habit are the first steps to a debt-free lifestyle.

Below are ways to tackle you debt.

1. Stop adding more debt

The rot stops here. Start differentiating between your good debts and bad ones. Recognise debt is good if it contributes to improving your financial situation over time. However, debts incurred to fund lifestyle expenses, like holidays or a designer wardrobe, are bad debts.

Sometimes, people confuse needs and wants. For example, you need a car for work but want a brand-new one. If you're borrowing to buy a car, the sensible move is to limit your debt and buy a second-hand vehicle.

Understanding the distinction between needs and wants will help you make more informed choices about when to borrow.

2. Set a budget to tackle your debts

If your debts become a problem, the proverbial ostrich head in the sand won't work. Problem debts escalate with procrastination and avoidance. Problem debts need action and urgency. You need to snap yourself out of hazardous spending habits and realise that debt is reducing your financial well-being.

Use Section 1 (Personal Budgeting) to help you monitor your income and outgoings. Your budgeting targets may need to be more aggressive when you are tackling your debt.

Keep a spending diary and challenge yourself to reduce your outgoings. A takeaway here, a car magazine there, a new skin cream and another T-shirt for the kids – the cost of these seemingly insignificant items adds up quickly.

Work out how to cut spending and use those savings to pay off your debts. If credit-card debt is affecting your life, you need to attack it.

3. Start tracking your debt reduction

You use Fitbits and other trackers to monitor your progress in improving your health metrics and you can also improve your financial health by tracking your efforts to reduce your debts.

There are downloadable tools for tracking money, debts, etc. You'll find calculators and payment schedules, all freely available online. If you feel comfortable with Excel, use Excel. If you're comfortable with a notepad, ruler and pen, then use them. Or use my version of the debt ladder below as a system for quickly reducing multiple debts (see p86).

But use something. Tracking is vital, and watching your debt chip away is motivating.

4. Set goals

To shed those extra pounds, we know we have to exercise and eat healthily. We have to change our behaviours and set goals to achieve anything new.

Setting a clear financial goal can motivate you to clear loans and stop you from getting deeper into debt. It doesn't matter what you want to achieve; it could be buying a house, saving for retirement or going on a world cruise. If you set a goal and keep your eye on the prize, it will keep you motivated. When you have a goal and a determination to save for it, you are less likely to be distracted by other 'wants' and accumulate bad debt.

5. Tell everyone

Be accountable to others in your debt reduction. Post your goals on social media and challenge yourself to reach them. Tell everyone you are giving yourself six months to clear your credit-card debt if that's a reasonable amount of time to achieve that goal. Identify an achievable goal to reduce debt, work towards it and share your progress. People will be supportive and are less likely to invite you on that expensive night out.

Finding other like-minded people on the same journey makes it easier. Share tips on how to reach your goals. It makes it harder for you to give up on your goals if you tell the world your plans.

6. Have an emergency fund

Save enough money for an emergency fund. When you start making an impact on your debts, start a small nest egg for unforeseen calamities. Sudden events can lead to sudden financial needs. Stop reaching for the credit card if the car breaks down or the boiler goes kaput. Setting aside some money each month to cover the cost of emergencies can help you avoid unplanned borrowing.

7. Start saving for larger purchases

Prioritise saving by using some of my tips in Section 1 (Personal Budgeting). When your short-term debts are cleared, work on allocating some income towards savings. Over time, these savings can fund larger purchases or investments, reducing your need to borrow. Stay away from credit cards and short-term loans when you clear them.

8. Adopt a more frugal mindset

Start living within your means and opt for a simpler lifestyle. Think twice before you buy, and reuse and recycle things like clothes and books. Join a library instead of buying books. Eating out and takeaways are expensive, so practising and expanding your cooking skills is an asset for any budget. Being frugal doesn't mean reducing your quality of life. It simply encourages wise and thoughtful spending and, in the case of home cooking, may be good for your health.

9. Learn more about finance

Financial literacy is an unknown subject in our schools and colleges, even though we're expected to handle finances every day. However, you're already well on your journey by picking up this book. By reading these sections, you will be equipped with greater knowledge about money and empowered to make better financial decisions.

The debt ladder

The debt ladder, or the debt avalanche method, is a strategy for paying off your debt. Usually, it's about listing your debts from the highest to lowest interest rate and tackling them in that order. You make minimum payments on all your debts except the largest. This is where you focus all your efforts.

My approach is a little different. I prefer to prioritise the smallest loans (in terms of amount owed) and tackle them first. This method enables you to see 'wins' more quickly. It keeps you motivated and encourages you to get out of debt faster. When the smallest loan is paid off, you concentrate all your debt repayment powers onto the next largest loan, and so on.

My debt ladder aims to tackle debts in manageable chunks and help you feel a sense of accomplishment after clearing a loan. You will feel motivated to continue as a result. This debt ladder strategy is practical and simple, and it works because it's about behaviour modification, not maths.

When you see the plan working, you stick to it. And when you do that, you'll succeed in becoming debt free.

How do I use the debt ladder?

Suppose you have four debt sources – a car loan, two credit-card debts and a loan from the credit union – that totals €17,000.

Your short-term repayments are €698 a month. List your loans in order of the biggest debt to the smallest – in this example the smallest is the credit-union loan of €2,000.

	LENDER	BALANCE (€)	PAYMENT (€)
1	Car loan	8,000.00	265.09
2	Credit card 1	4,000.00	200.00
3	Credit card 2	3,000.00	133.23
4	Credit union	2,000.00	100.00
	Totals	17,000.00	698.32

Using the debt ladder strategy, you restructure your repayments as follows:

- Reduce your monthly repayments on all the debts except for the credit-union loan, so that every month you now pay the minimum on three of your loans.
- You continue to pay €698 into your monthly debt repayments, but the extra money now goes towards clearing the credit-union debt. See the new payment structure on the right below.

	LENDER	BALANCE (€)	PAYMENT (€)	NEW PAYMENT (€)
1	Car loan	8,000.00	265.09	100.00
2	Credit card 1	4,000.00	200.00	100.00
3	Credit card 2	3,000.00	133.23	70.00
4	Credit union	2,000.00	100.00	428.32
	Totals	17,000.00	698.32	698.32

- By directing the maximum amount to your smallest debt, you pay off this debt far more quickly. The loan is paid in less than five months rather than twenty.

	LENDER	BALANCE (€)	PAYMENT (€)	NEW PAYMENT (€)
1	Car loan	8,000.00	265.09	100.00
2	Credit card 1	4,000.00	200.00	100.00
3	Credit card 2	3,000.00	133.23	498.32
4	~~Credit union~~	~~2,000.00~~	~~100.00~~	~~00.00~~
	Totals	15,000.00	598.32	698.32

- When you pay off the credit union, you focus on the credit-card debt of €3,000, which should be cleared in just over six months with the new payment structure.
- Congratulations – within eleven months, you have cleared two debts.
- After that, keep the momentum and roll the repayments into the following loan. You'll clear the big car loan in a year now that you're concentrating all your monthly €698 debt repayment capacity just on that loan.

	LENDER	BALANCE (€)	PAYMENT (€)	NEW PAYMENT (€)
1	Car loan	8,000.00	265.09	698.32
2	~~Credit card 1~~	~~4,000.00~~	~~200.00~~	~~00.00~~
3	~~Credit card 2~~	~~3,000.00~~	~~133.23~~	~~00.00~~
4	~~Credit union~~	~~2,000.00~~	~~100.00~~	~~00.00~~
	Totals	8,000.00	265.09	698.32

Progress is rapid with my version of the debt ladder. And when you see the plan is working, you stick to it. When the debts are clear, you have €698 a month, which you can save or invest for your future.

- Please note you may need to negotiate with your creditors to utilise this debt ladder.
- Also, note that any restructuring agreed with your creditors may affect your credit record with the Central Credit Register. Also, some of the larger loans may take longer to pay off. (This is not a one-size-fits-all solution, so adjust the ladder to suit your needs best.)

How can I clear my credit-card debt?

People often ask me how to tackle credit-card debt because this often becomes a problem debt for people.

It's easy to fall into the credit-card debt trap because the 'buy now, pay later' approach seems easy. Our brains are wired to respond positively to instant gratification, making us cannon fodder for credit cards. Credit cards are like casinos; they want to keep you at the table. They prefer if you keep spending and pay minimum amounts on your debts for protracted periods.

I'm also reminded of a scene in the TV series *The Sopranos* where Tony Soprano's nephew, Christopher, explains loan sharking to a wannabe gangster. I'm paraphrasing here: 'When you bleed a guy, don't squeeze him dry right away … So you can bleed him again and again.'

The credit-card companies won't thank me for that mafia

comparison, but the problem with credit cards is that their debt charges are excessively high.

AIB had an attractive 8.5% rate for some credit-card customers, but that was over a decade ago. Reasonable credit-card rates are rare now, with most interest rates ranging from 14–23% annually.

And that's compounding interest. With compound interest, interest is charged on interest from the previous month. So, the longer it takes to clear your balance, the more you'll pay in compound interest. Credit-card rates are exceedingly high.

Credit cards are a great tool if you clear your balance on time every month. However, many people cannot do this, so credit-card companies make a lot of money. Here is the smartest way to eliminate your credit-card debt – stop using your credit card.

Yes, I hear you. 'Thanks for making me read this section to tell me something so obvious.' However, if you have problem debt on your credit cards, you may have a behavioural problem or addiction to using credit cards.

Below are a few more tips to reduce your credit-card debt:

1. Stop feeding the habit and adding to your debt. Cash is king. Make a weekly budget and pay for everything in cash. Make the cash last until the end of the week. Alternatively, transfer the same money to a Revolut card and live within that budget.

   Use interest-free balance transfers. Try transferring the debt to a card that offers interest-free balance transfers for new customers. This is a smart move as you could get six months to a year of interest-free credit – saving you hundreds of euro in interest while you clear the debt. This space may give you the opportunity to clear a credit-card debt without paying compounding interest rates.

2. The Competition and Consumer Protection Commission (CCPC) compares cards and lists those offering interest-free balance transfers. Only do this if you're committed to paying off the debt within the introductory low-interest-rate window. Otherwise, your interest rates could become even higher than the card you left.

3. Get a low-interest loan from a credit union or bank. Then clear your high-interest credit-card debt, cut up your credit card and clear that lower-interest loan.

4. Reduce your credit-card limit. The credit-card companies love to see you spend and often automatically increase your credit limit. A smaller credit limit will stop you from overspending and help slow down the rate at which you build up debt.

5. Contact your credit-card company for a lower interest rate. This seems blindingly obvious, but few people do it. Often, a simple phone call to the issuer is all it takes to get a reduced rate – especially if you are a long-term customer who makes payments on time. If you see a lower rate by a competitor, tell the customer services, and there's a chance they'll match the offer.

6. Cut expenses and divert the savings to pay off your debts. (See below.)

My Top Ten tips for cutting back on daily expenses

Always start with your budgeting plan and an accurate list of your income and outgoings. Before reading about cutting out and budgeting below, it's important to note this is not something I want readers to do long term. I want you to come away from *Money Made Easy* with a more confident approach to your money. However, if you're struggling to manage your debt and you want to get out of debt quickly, you need to watch every cent, so cut costs and redirect money to pay off debts.

Cutting costs doesn't feel good in the short term, but you'll feel great in the long run when you become debt free.

Below are some easy ways to cut expenses.

1. Make your morning coffee at home, bring your lunch to work and stop buying bottled water. Then, divert those savings to clear your debts.

2. Consider cutting out the gym subscription and spinning classes and taking free online classes instead. You may miss the social aspects of exercise for a few months, but you won't lose out on the health benefits. Thousands of classes and workouts are available for free on YouTube and various apps. Don't forget to divert the savings to clear your debts.

3. Compare utility providers and ensure you get the best gas, electricity, phone and broadband deals. You often don't even have to change providers. Tell your provider about the deal you can get elsewhere, and they will often meet it. Again, divert the savings to clear your debts.

4.   Challenge yourself to reduce the use of utilities. Hang out the washing instead of running a dryer. Turn down the thermostat on your water or heating by a degree or two. Ensure you use a timer for your heating and try reducing the use by an hour. Only use energy-saving bulbs. Use the air fryer, slow cooker or microwave instead of the oven. Put clothes into colder, shorter wash cycles when possible. Notice the savings in the bills? Divert the savings to clear your debts.

5.   Stop leaking cash on monthly subscriptions for television, music, books and various streaming services. I see clients with dozens of subscriptions. Individually, the payments start small but mount until they cost hundreds of euros a year. Look at each one and ask yourself: 'How much do I use this? Can I live without it? Can I downgrade to a cheaper service?' Divert any savings to your debts.

6.   Look for opportunities to increase your income. Do you have a spare room to let? Could you mind pets in your spare time? Advertise in your local vet's practice or sign up for petsittersIreland.com, pawshake.ie or catinaflat.ie. Do you have a car-parking space or a driveway you can rent? (See parkpnp.com or daft.ie.) Can you find part-time work? Divert new earnings to clear your debts.

7.   Groceries are a considerable cost in every household. Raid your cupboards and use what you have before you shop. Then, challenge yourself to become more savvy at shopping. Reduce expensive waste by making a meal list for the week and writing your shopping list accordingly.

Irish people are well known for their loyalty to overpriced premium brands, which the supermarkets stock at eye level. Look to products on the lower shelves for the best prices instead. Plan your shopping, stick to the shopping list and don't stray into middle-aisle purchases.

8. Eat at home. Forget about takeaways and restaurants – for a few months, at least. Don't feel confident in the kitchen? There's no excuse. Learn the skills you need for free on YouTube. Divert your savings on eating out or takeaways to your debts.

9. House insurance, car insurance, health insurance, life insurance and mortgage repayments – check them all. Compare products with other suppliers and see where you can make savings. Add those savings to clear your debts.

10. Cash in on a massive clear-out and use the proceeds to clear your debts. Get your unwanted clothes, designer duds and household items on Depop, eBay, Luxury Exchange, Facebook Marketplace and DoneDeal.

What is lifestyle creep?

I meet people who say they're broke, even though they received a big bonus and a raise just months earlier. I ask, where's that extra €400 a month disappearing to? And they look at me blankly.

These vanishing earnings are often referred to as 'lifestyle creep' or 'lifestyle inflation'. Our standards of living rise to meet our salaries. Suddenly, what we once regarded as a luxury is now seen as a necessity. The extra money is used to fund a more expensive lifestyle rather than increasing our savings or investments.

Beware of lifestyle creep. Set goals for saving and investing, and do not get into debt with borrowing. Reverse engineer this behaviour and start cutting back on expenses.

CLIENT CASE
ANTONI, AGED 30

Anotoni came in for a consultation to start an investment account. I see a lot of younger guys who are interested in investing because there's a perception that investing is 'sexy'. Investing was the preserve of old banker types, but now there's a level of prestige in it. Who'd have thought investment funds would be cool? Anyway, Antoni wanted to start investing. Unfortunately, he had multiple short-term, personal, credit-union and car-finance loans. He was meeting all his repayments and had a monthly cash surplus, but we had to advise him against investing.

We explained that the interest on his loans was 8%. He'd be lucky if he got a 6–8% return on the investments. In real terms, he might make 4% after exit tax and a management charge. So why chase 4% when you can save 8%? It was clear he should use his extra income to reduce his loans.

It made sense to him when we explained it. He went off, returned a year later and used the money he had been spending on his short-term debts to invest.

What are the different forms of debt?

Secured debt

This debt is where you pledge an asset (like your house or car) as collateral. It's like saying, 'If I can't repay the loan, you can take the car or house instead.' Mortgages and car loans are examples of secured debt. The bank seizes the collateral – takes your home or car – to recoup its losses if you fail to make repayments.

Unsecured debt

This type of debt doesn't have any collateral backing it. Credit-card debt and personal loans are examples of unsecured debt. You might, for instance, buy clothes on your credit card and get a new kitchen with a personal loan. These only have value to you. The bank has no pledged asset to seize if you cannot pay the loans. As a result, these loans carry higher interest rates, which acts like extra insurance for the lender.

Revolving debt

Think of it as a cycle – you borrow, you pay some back. Then, you borrow some more up to your credit limit. Credit cards are the most common form of revolving debt. Bank overdrafts are another. You can borrow and repay up to your credit limit, offering great flexibility.

Instalment debt

Instalment debt consists of a loan for a fixed amount that you repay in fixed amounts, or instalments, over time. Car loans, personal loans and mortgages are instalment debts. You usually sign a contract to pay the same monthly amount until the debt is fully repaid.

Personal Contract Plans and Hire Purchase

Over the past decade, Personal Contract Plans (PCP) have become common in Ireland. I am not particularly enamoured with this form of debt.

A hire purchase (HP) or PCP agreement is a credit agreement. You hire an item, usually a car with a PCP, and pay an agreed amount monthly. But there are some things you need to know about PCPs.

- You do not own the car until the final payment, which may take five years. You are hiring the vehicle from the finance company until the contract ends.

- This lack of ownership means you don't build equity in the car and don't have the option to sell it to recoup some value.

- Many PCP or HP agreements have a 'balloon' payment at the end of the contract. This is usually bigger than the monthly payment. You pay this, and then you own the vehicle. You could also return the car to the finance company or you can roll over the contract for a new PCP agreement.

- The contractual arrangement ends at this point, but the car owner is often encouraged to roll into another follow-on PCP agreement. As a result, these contracts and financial obligations continue for years.

- There can be sizeable early termination penalties if you end the agreement before the agreed-upon contract period. This can be a major headache if you no longer need or can afford the vehicle.

- If you do not keep up the repayments, they can seize the car as part of the PCP agreement.
- PCP agreements are based on the predicted future values of the car. However, if the actual value depreciates more than expected, you may face negative equity at the end of the contract. If the car's value is lower than the agreed-upon future value, you pay this difference.
- As a final sticking point, there are other restrictions to PCP contracts, such as mileage limits, servicing obligations and charges for 'excessive' wear and tear.

Overdrafts

Overdrafts are a banking facility that enables account holders to withdraw more money from their accounts than they have available. In simple terms, it's like borrowing money from the bank through your current account.

Overdraft facilities from the main banks can often be switched on via their apps. If you apply for an overdraft, you'll face little resistance – banks often give instant approval. Banks love overdrafts because they're good for them. However, they're not always so good for their customers.

Overdrafts usually range from €500 to €10,000. Like all debt, overdrafts make you more reliant on debt and gobble up your salary.

Let's say you have a bad month and avail of your overdraft. At the end of the following month, you expect to be paid €3,200, but your balance is €2,500 because your overdraft gets sorted first. This may not be enough for the month, so you are in a continual overdraft situation.

While overdrafts can be convenient in certain situations, they can also negatively affect your finances. Here's why:

- The fees, interest and charges are high. They only charge you on what you use, but ranges are typically 11%–15%. Anytime you see an interest rate north of 5%, you should shudder and back away. Overdraft fees and charges can quickly add up, making it an expensive way to borrow money.

- Overdrafts contribute to a debt spiral. Continuous borrowing through overdrafts results in a perpetually negative balance. They make it difficult to get out of the cycle of debt.

- Some leading bank apps even display a false current account balance that includes your overdraft limit. This isn't your money. It is misleading and unethical in my view. This balance comes with a baked-in interest rate that is constantly eating away at your money.

- Overdrafts are another temptation to overspend. It's easy to overspend and rely on borrowed money rather than living within your means. An overdraft creates a false sense of available funds, leading to impulsive purchases.

- Constantly relying on overdrafts can make it difficult to break the cycle of living from pay packet to pay packet and can lead to a lack of financial security in the long run.

Personal loans and the importance of APR

Rates for car loans, home-improvement loans and personal loans from banks, An Post and credit unions will typically range from 6%–12%.

Credit unions can have higher interest rates than a retail bank or post office. The trade-off may be easier access and a more flexible repayment schedule. Some may be willing to pay a slightly higher loan rate for this.

Credit unions link your loan amount to your 'shares' or savings. Union members may like the idea of keeping a cushion of savings in the credit union and getting a loan based on these savings. However, money on deposit in the credit union often earns 0%. It makes more sense to use your savings than taking out a loan at a charge of 10% or more.

See the example below of borrowing from a credit union.

Loan amount	€30,000
Loan duration	5 years

Each credit union sets its own interest rates at local level. Your actual interest rate may vary from the average and max figures below, depending on your credit union.

AVERAGE CREDIT UNION LOAN RATE	
Average loan interest rate	10.59% APR
Monthly repayments	€646.16
Total interest to be paid	€8,769.32
Total amount repayable	€38,769.32

The APR refers to the annual percentage rate or the yearly interest the borrowers pay. Understanding the cost of credit is important. This credit union loan calculator shows the price of €30,000 over five years at a 10.59% APR rate. The total cost to the borrower is €8,769. Please note that each credit union sets its own interest rates, and this is for illustration purposes only.

Another example from a bank illustrates the savings made by borrowing the same money at a slightly lower APR. This five-year loan of €30,0000 has an APR of 8.95%. Even though the difference in APR is only 1.64%, the repayment to the bank is €7,017.00. This is €1,752.32 cheaper than the same loan with 10.59% APR.

This shows the value of shopping around for better interest rates.

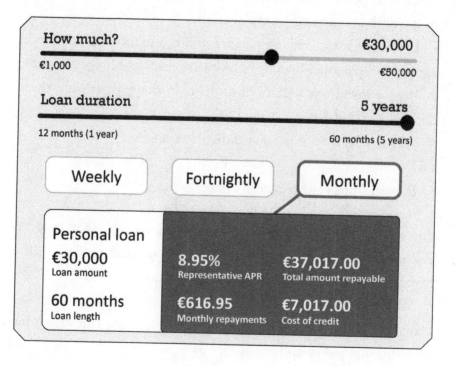

However, my advice will always be never to fund home improvements or cars through debt. Use savings and excess cash, and if you don't have the savings now, wait until you do.

If you are unfortunate enough to get sick or injured, ideally you have that income protection or illness cover policy we'll discuss in Section 5 (Financial Protection).

What happens to debt after death?

It's often the case that one person takes the lead regarding financial affairs in a couple. I see it all the time with my clients. One person is the financially literate one who sorts out all the bills and knows where everything is. We all have our strengths and weaknesses, and this is perfectly normal. However, neither partner should be in the dark about their financial affairs.

If you are the surviving partner and are named on any credit agreement, personal loan or bill, you are responsible for the debt.

If your loved one had a bill or debts in their name only, these debts will either be:

• Written off if your partner didn't have assets.

OR

• Repaid from your partner's estate.

An estate can be property, savings, pensions, etc. that may be due to you via estate planning, inheritance or after probate. Life-insurance policies may form part of the estate.

When mourning the loss of a loved one, the last thing you want is financial problems. And sensible planning can save a lot of additional worry and stress.

If your loved one has a will, the beneficiaries receive their inheritance after the deceased's debts are cleared. Remember, a basic will costs €100 to €200 and can save a lot of heartache for those who survive us.

If you die without making a will, your estate is distributed between your surviving family in the way set out in law rather than in the manner you may have intended. Make a will if you want a say over who inherits your estate.

The final word on debt

If you have a debt problem, don't overanalyse how you got there. Don't blame yourself or others. Recognise the negative patterns that brought you to the place you are, remedy them, and move on.

Clearing debt can be daunting, but a shift in perspective will impact how you face the issue. It's not about how much you owe but about how you handle it that matters. Debt may be a looming presence in your life today, but with determination and strategic action, it doesn't have to define your future.

Sleepless nights and fear ebb away when you take positive steps to tackle debt. As you chip away, you'll no longer see debt as an insurmountable mountain. As you succeed in clearing one debt and then another, you'll realise you have the power to conquer this problem.

I hope this debt section will empower you to take your first steps towards a future free from bad debt. The journey ahead may not be easy but stick to the steps and the tips I outlined above. If you do, you'll retrain your mindset and gain money-management skills that will transform your financial well-being and future for ever.

CLIENT CASE

SIMON, AGED 37

When we met Simon, he was in a spiral of debt. He and his partner wanted to get on the property ladder, but he held them back with his debts.

He had a large car and personal loans and made minimal payments on sizeable credit-card debts. His earnings were a healthy €3,600 a month net, but he was spending €1,100 in monthly loan repayments and hardly making a dent in his borrowings.

To fast track the debt reduction process, he agreed to sell his car and buy an older one. He also moved most of his credit-card debt to a new card with an introductory 0% interest rate. Then, he started clearing the personal loan, sold the car and repaid the car loan. He cleared those before the 0% interest term on the credit card ended and piled all his efforts into tackling that.

When he'd cleared his debts, he began saving the same €1,100 a month – a hefty €13,200 a year – towards the mortgage deposit the couple needed. As soon as he cleared his debts, we reminded him he was increasing his own wealth rather than the bank's profit margins.

Your 7-point action plan for managing debt

- Critically assess your financial situation. List all your debts, including the amount owed, interest rate, minimum payments and the due date.
- Create a budget. Develop a realistic budget that includes all your income and expenses. Now include a portion for settling your debts. Keep money aside for emergencies.
- Prioritise your debts. Mortgage debt is more important than other types of debt. If you are having problems meeting that repayment, speak with your lender as a matter of urgency.
- Negotiate with or change lenders as part of a new plan. Renegotiate payment terms. Ask if they can reduce your interest rate. See if you can switch credit cards and transfer your balance to an introductory no-interest loan.
- Consider consolidating your debts if dealing with multiple high-interest credit-card debt. This can lower your interest rate and simplify your finances with one monthly payment.
- Create a proper payment plan. Try to pay the minimum on all your debts, but focus on paying off one debt in particular. When that debt is paid off, move on to the next one.

- Seek professional help from an organisation such as Money Advice and Budgeting Service (MABS) if you feel overwhelmed by your debts. They can assist with a budgeting plan and help you with money management. They may even negotiate lower interest rates and better terms with your lenders.

SECTION 3
SAVING AND INVESTING

Many people in Ireland believe investing is for high rollers who have stockbrokers and read *Bloomberg News*. In fact, lots of Irish people are already investors and don't know it.

What is investing?

Investing is not that complicated. Investments are types of 'valuables' that people buy and hold, hoping that they will grow in value over time. These valuables are called 'assets' and include equities (stocks and shares), bonds, property, cash, and commodities like oil, gas, gold and silver. However, anything that holds value is an asset. A house is an asset. Cash in your wallet is an asset.

Of course, not all assets are equal. Some assets will depreciate – for example, most cars devalue as they age. Other assets, such as property or equities, will increase in value over time. You can also hold a valuable asset but never realise it. For example, you're unlikely to 'cash in' your family home.

An investor is any person who puts money into any of these assets in the expectation of achieving a profit. The aim of buying most assets is to hold them for a period and then sell them for a profit or 'return' on your investment.

Being an investor simply means putting money in more places than your current account or savings account. For example, anyone in Ireland with a pension is already an investor, as most pension funds are invested in many of the assets mentioned above.

Some assets can produce regular income for investors. Investing in property, for example, produces rent as income. Investing in shares and equities can provide dividends (a payment made by a company to shareholders from the business profits).

When assets increase in value, we talk about 'appreciation' or 'capital growth' for investors.

Why should we invest?

Investing is about protecting your income and wealth and putting your money to work for you. When you make good investments, your wealth grows.

Money left under the mattress or in zero- or low-interest accounts devalues because of inflation. Investing is all about combating or outpacing the effects of inflation. We talk more about inflation below.

Instead of investing, many Irish people are in the habit of

holding 'pockets' of financial assets here, there and everywhere. They may have €20,000 in the credit union, an old pension worth €60,000 from an old job and a few thousand sitting in a current account that's never used. People often have money and resources idling in accounts they have forgotten about. Even though they're not millionaires, by not investing their money, they fail to make it work for them.

Despite what people may think, investing is not about getting rich. Investing is about beating inflation and making your money work for you. If you have cash sitting in an Irish bank account with 2% interest and inflation is running at 6%, your money has just devalued by 4%.

Of course, if you invest in the right assets and don't need access to your money for a long time, you may become 'rich' – but that's an added perk of investing. Your primary aim is to beat inflation.

When should I invest?

The best starting point before investing is to understand your financial situation thoroughly.

My first job as a financial planner is to consider how much disposable income you have and what level of short-term debt you have. Have you cleared your credit cards or other short-term loans?

After that, I'll ask if you have an emergency fund – a minimum of €1,000 (more if you're self-employed) in a savings account somewhere like a credit union. My next question is if you have short-term savings for expected expenses, such as holidays, weddings, Christmas, a house deposit, etc.

I'll also ask if you have insurance coverage to provide an income should you be out of work because of an accident or illness.

If your answer is no to any of the above, my advice will be it's not time to invest.

I want to see you create a safety net before you invest. In my experience, most investors fail because they're not set up to succeed. Regardless of asset class, investments will go up and down in value. And you lose if you're forced to take money out when markets are down.

So, my advice for successful investing is straightforward: *Don't invest all your money.* Have money aside in the emergency fund and have income protection. Don't invest cash you might need back in a few years. Only invest for the long term – five years or more.

I often see people making a big push and they invest everything. Then there's an economic downturn and suddenly they lose their jobs or their income drops, and they need urgent access to their investment. Typically, when economic trends are down, so are most investment markets. This scenario is a nightmare. We have someone with all their money in markets, but they need access when the markets are at their lowest. If this person had only kept a decent cash reserve, they could have given their investments time to recover from the negative position.

Quiz

Are you ready to invest?

- Are you budgeting correctly and reaching the end of the month with some money in your account?

- Have you cleared your high-interest, short-term debt?
- Do you have an adequate emergency fund?
- Do you have surplus income over debt and cash savings?
- Have you established your monthly costs and know what money you can afford to put away for five years or more?
- Do you have income protection?
- Do you have a goal for investing?

If the answer is no to any of these questions, please pause your investment plans and reconsider your options. If your reply is yes, investing is your logical next stage.

I'm not rich; can I be an investor?

You don't need €1 million to be an investor. You don't need €5,000 a month. You can start investing with as little as €100 a month.

One of the askpaul brand's core values is to make investing accessible for everyone. From the day I started, my aim was to empower everyone to improve their financial circumstances. I try to show people they can invest and grow their money regardless of their bank balance.

Whether you're Mary with €1 million to invest or Bob with €100 doesn't really matter – the investment advice is the same and the return is the same. The only difference is with a 10% gain, Mary will make €100,000 and Bob will make €10. But the fundamentals are the same – they will both make a 10% gain.

Don't be afraid to start small and build a small nest egg. I hear so many people say, 'Sure, it's not worth getting 10% when I'm only saving €100.' But if you do that every month for twenty or thirty years, you become like Mary – Mary, the millionaire, had to start somewhere as well.

I've helped some people invest millions, from Lotto winners to business tycoons, and I've also helped people on social welfare. Everyone can invest. The askpaul brand is about creating an equal playing field for people from all walks of life to invest and grow their wealth.

CLIENT CASE
SEAN, AGED 62

A new client called Sean came to us. He was concerned after checking a pension plan he had taken out years ago. He was nearing pension age and discovered it wasn't worth near what he expected.

'I've got a pittance in my pension plan,' he told me. 'I paid in for years and I'm getting nothing back.'

I checked his pension and had to say to him, 'You paid in €80 a month, you're getting back €140 a month. That's a good return.'

It wasn't the pension fund's fault – he just hadn't funded it enough. I come across people like Sean all the time. Sometimes, I have to remind clients a pension is not a magic tree. You have to fund your pension properly. And you must be realistic about funding and the returns.

What is the difference between saving and investing?

Irish people are known as a nation of savers, with our funds held on deposit in banks, building societies and credit unions. Banks pay you for the use of your money and this payment is called 'interest'. However, most of these institutions offer minimal return, meaning most savers receive little or no interest on their savings.

To get higher interest rates, you often must agree to restricted access to your money. Some banks have a twelve-month notice deposit account offering 2% interest. In return, you must leave your money with the bank for a year, limiting your access.

Bank deposit accounts provide security rather than profits to savers. Under the Deposit Guarantee Scheme in Ireland, up to €100,000 of your savings are protected if the bank fails. Many are happy to get a 2% return to have the security of the government guarantee scheme behind their cash.

Deposit accounts have a place. They provide a useful short-term option for access to immediate cash. A deposit account is fine for financial goals like saving for your summer holiday or paying for a deposit on a house in the coming years.

Personally, I have an affinity for credit unions in this situation. I like them for their customer-based service and community ethos. However, like banks, credit unions are only acceptable as a short-term option. They are not the place for medium- to long-term storage of your funds as your money will decrease in value.

The problem is that receiving 2% interest on your money is not enough to keep up with the current inflation rate or the rising cost of living. As a result, the value of your savings is almost always eroding in a deposit account.

People should also understand how banking works. Some seem to think the bank holds your money in some vast vault. Instead, the banks do something you should ... they put the money to work for them.

Banks either invest money or lend it to your neighbour for 8% on a car loan, 4% on a mortgage or 21% on a credit card. They use *your* money to make money. We all leave school in Ireland with little or no financial education. It means we don't learn how money works and more importantly how to make it work better for us.

How do I make money grow?

On p113 is a graph showing the gross returns for four savings and investment accounts from 1993 to 2023.

If you started investing €250 per month in an investment with an 8% return in 1993, you would have €372,453 gross in that account by 2023.

If you put the same amount into a savings account with a 2% interest rate, you would have €127,247 over the same thirty years.

Of course, this is gross interest before taxes and charges, which we will discuss later. This graph focuses on the vast contrast in growth between the various interest rates. The difference compound interest makes over time is amazing.

COMPOUND INTEREST ON YOUR MONEY

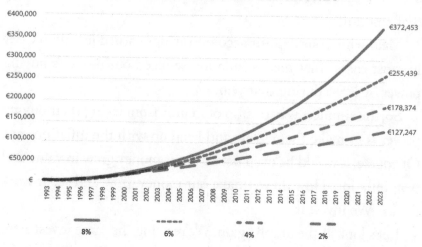

Compound interest is a bit like a snowball rolling down a hill. As it goes, it gathers more and more snow until it becomes an avalanche. You start with some money (a small snowball). You earn interest (add snow) on it and the money ball gets bigger. Then that bigger ball of money earns more interest, and so on. That's how your money can grow significantly over time with compound interest – it's a financial snowball effect.

What is inflation?

People in their thirties and forties will remember their parents talking about buying houses for £20,000 in old Irish punts or buying a pint for £1. Well, folks, prices today are much higher because of inflation.

Inflation is the gradual – or sometimes dramatic – rise in prices over time, eroding your money's purchasing power. Inflation rates vary from year to year. In Ireland, the inflation rate in 2022 was over 8%, meaning prices of everyday goods rose on average by that amount.

Meanwhile, our deposit account savings earned less than 0.5% in most cases. That means inflation reduced our money's buying power by 7.5% during that year.

So, the simplest way to stop our euros from losing their buying power is to make them grow and keep up with the inflation rate. Of course, it would be even better if our money grew in value and beat inflation. How do we make our money grow and see it work for us? We invest it.

Let's look at the graph again. We're using the same investment figure of €250 per month. However, this time, I've adjusted the investment return downwards by 2% to account for inflation.

COMPOUND INTEREST ON YOUR MONEY

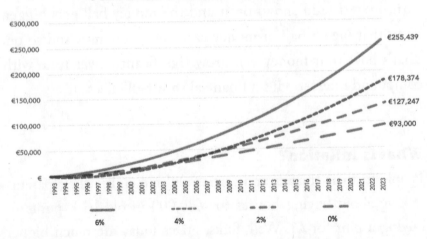

Look at the difference now. Inflation's impact on the 8% return has reduced €372,453 to real growth of €255,439. That's a difference of €117,014. Of course, there's a way to beat that 2% inflation – by increase your €250 per month payments by 2% each year. Then, your investment keeps up with inflation. That slight annual increase would have added €117,014 to the value of your money.

However, there are degrees of risk with investing. The value of an asset can also decrease or even be wiped out – like Irish bank shares during the post-2008 financial crash. As a result, the financial industry talks about assessing clients' 'risk tolerance' before choosing investments.

What is risk tolerance?

'Risk tolerance' is a loaded and subjective term. In the financial industry, it refers to an individual's willingness to take on risk when making investment decisions. It assesses a person's tolerance for potential losses in pursuit of potential gains.

Risk tolerance and the capacity to bear risk are two different things. I believe using risk tolerance questionnaires as a guide for financial planners is flawed. Some of you will have already gone through this risk tolerance exercise with a bank, planner or online. You'll have completed these questionnaires of varying lengths to end up on a scale of one to seven. If you score one, you are ultra-conservative and have a low risk tolerance. If you score seven, you have a high risk tolerance and will risk a lot, if not everything, in pursuit of a profit.

In isolation, this is a lazy and dangerous methodology for assessing how to invest your money. The problem is that those new to investing may not clearly understand the risks involved or the consequences of those risks.

Using risk-tolerance questionnaires is a paint-by-numbers

form of investment analysis. Yes, risk tolerance should form part of the conversation, but it should not be the only part when discussing what you invest in and for how long.

There is danger in being reckless, but there is also danger in being too conservative.

If you have experienced this casual box-ticking attitude from a planner, please get a new financial planner. Real financial professionals will not rely on these tick-box guides. They will assess your goals properly and provide risk-management strategies.

It's like building the foundations of a house. If you start the wrong way, it's only a matter of time before things go very bad indeed.

CLIENT CASE
ANGELA, AGED 57

Angela scored a six on a risk tolerance test, indicating a high-risk tolerance. She had €400,000 to invest. However, it would have been wrong to choose an investment strategy for her based on these results alone.

Yes, she was a risk taker, but when we discussed her goals, she wanted to retire when she turned sixty. She also had no other savings and a small mortgage.

In this case, she had to approach risk more cautiously, and her risk tolerance needed to be adjusted downwards. She was willing to make risky investment decisions but hadn't fully considered her circumstances and the potential downsides.

CLIENT CASE

NOELLE, AGED 31

Noelle wanted to put €300 a month into a regular premium pension plan. When I checked her risk tolerance while setting up a pension, she emerged with a conservative rating of two. However, she had thirty-five years left to work, so she had more than thirty years to grow her money and overcome volatility.

In this case, I saw it as my job to encourage her to adjust her risk tolerance upwards. She was a naturally cautious investor, but she needed to consider her life circumstances and the fact that she had time on her side. She could afford to be more aggressive in her investment strategy.

How do I reduce the risks of investing?

There are no guarantees with investments. Investing always comes with the risk of losing some or all of your money.

If you invest in shares, for example, they will rise in value when the company is doing well and fall when it is doing poorly. However, there are strategies to minimise loss.

1. Diversification

You've heard the adage, 'Don't put all your eggs in one basket.' Well, I give the same advice when investing. Don't put all your money in one asset or one investment category. Diversification refers to spreading investments across many types of assets to help reduce your risk.

For example, the 2008 financial crisis was a catastrophe because so many had invested their fortunes in property. People thought that buying several apartments with 100% mortgages was a smart move. They thought property prices were going to rise for ever.

Of course, that didn't happen and property prices crashed, as they inevitably do after a boom. As a result, many individuals, construction companies and banks were left in financial ruin.

Similarly, many people considered bank shares wise and safe investments. They poured their life savings into Anglo-Irish Bank and other banks' shares with disastrous results when the institutions failed or their share price plummeted. Many Irish people lost everything because they hadn't diversified their investments.

Diversification is essential for good investing. For example, shares may plunge in value during a global financial crisis. However, the savvier investor has diversified and also has assets in bonds and gold. While the stocks and shares fall in value, the bonds or gold investments usually rise as investors flock to 'safer' investments. Buying across all asset classes means spreading your risk. It also means losses and gains are more balanced, and your wealth is protected. If you want to invest in a single asset long term, i.e. equities in your pension fund, you should make sure your fund is diversified across different sectors and geographical regions.

2. Time

When it comes to safe investing, the most valuable tool is time. I always tell clients they need a medium- to long-term time horizon of five years or more.

All assets have ups and downs, good years and bad years – but investing has been around for centuries.

People have placed their money into different assets or investments to beat rising inflation for hundreds of years. And history can teach us a lot. Economies are cyclical, rising and falling over the years. The stock markets soar in a bull market and fall in a bear market. However, economies inevitably recover. Investors who hold their nerve will see many of their investments rise over the long term.

However, if you have a narrow investment timeframe, you are more vulnerable to sudden and unpredictable changes in the market. Time gives your investments the chance to recover from inevitable fluctuations in the economy.

When you are confident that your portfolio is well managed and diversified, trust the process and let the money do its thing. My mantra is: 'Invest and forget …'

Sitting on your investments for long periods is the best way to see your wealth grow. It is not *timing the market* but *time in the markets* that will bear fruits for your money over the medium to long term.

How long should I invest?

As I've said above, I always advise clients they need a medium- to long-term mindset before starting a journey in investment. Your investment time horizon should be five or more years, preferably ten or more, with an average growth of ideally 4–5%. Investments may achieve higher growth in particularly good years; I've see years of 20%+ growth. The longer you invest, the more time you have to ride out short-term market drops. Patience is a virtue when it comes to investing.

Yes, as financial planners we do yearly reviews, sometimes more. We also issue investment reports and performance charts, and sometimes we adjust our investment strategies, but we don't react to short-term blips.

What is the minimum I can invest?

A sustainable amount you can commit to every single month is probably more important than a minimum amount. However, I recommend a minimum of €100 a month for investment funds.

You can also pay into an investment fund with a lump sum. When investing a large lump sum, my advice is to drip-feed it into funds over six to twelve months. This enables you to average out the purchase price over time, potentially reducing the impact of market fluctuations. It may help you avoid buying at a high point in the market.

However, the minimum required depends on the asset in which you want to invest. Buying property, for example, will require a far more significant investment. Property investing requires a 30% lump sum for a deposit followed by monthly mortgage payments.

If you go the DIY route using investment apps, no minimum amount of money is required.

How do I invest?

A large assortment of financial institutions and professionals are available to invest for you.

Financial planners or financial brokers

Because investing involves risk, it's vital to take advice before making any decision. Investments have long-term implications for your life. Consulting an impartial financial planner is the first step towards making a safe and informed choice.

Life-assurance companies

Life-assurance companies such as Zurich Life, New Ireland, Standard Life, Aviva Life & Pensions and Irish Life offer many policies and asset classes for growing your savings. The choice is so vast it can be bewildering and overwhelming. Comparing the fee and commission structures can also be a virtual maze. Always seek professional financial advice.

Banks

Major banks in Ireland have divisions that provide savings and investment services. You can approach banks and enquire about their offerings and invest in them. However, banks are usually 'tied agents', meaning they act on behalf of their financial institution and so are limited to offering that institution's products. Also, as tied agents, their primary responsibility is to work in the bank's best interests rather than yours.

Another hazard warning – banks' products may also come with high commission rates, which may erode your investments over the years.

Stockbrokers

In Ireland, licensed stockbrokers can help you buy various investment options, including stocks, shares and bonds. They have a wide range of options depending on your investment goals. However, the stockbroker industry tends to be aimed at higher net-worth clients.

Government bonds

Many people invest or save in Irish Government Bonds or Irish Sovereign Bonds. These bonds are typically available for purchase directly from the National Treasury Management Agency (NTMA) or through authorised financial institutions. The NTMA's website provides information on their bond offerings and how to invest in them. They are considered safe, but the interest rates are typically low.

Online trading platforms

Several online platforms offer bond trading services, enabling you to buy and sell investments electronically. You can access these platforms from your computer or mobile device. However, online trading should come with a big flashing red light. Firstly, ensure that your chosen platform is reputable and regulated. Many people using these services lack the knowledge or experience to make informed investing decisions. Nevertheless, these new investors, often called 'retail investors', are rapidly increasing in number.

Who are the new investors or 'retail investors'?

If the stock market was ever the preserve of the wealthy, that day is over. The finance industry has undergone a massive transformation in the last ten years with the rise of trading apps and new investors.

These new investors, often known as retail investors, are armed with a growing number of these trading apps and new platforms like Revolut and eToro. Robinhood was one of the first to arrive in 2013 and is now a large US investment app with over 12 million retail users. Many invest in stocks and shares with as much ease as they share content on social media. In fact, 'investing' has become something of a cultural phenomenon among a growing number of people.

I use the word 'investing' advisably because I believe many retail investors will probably lose their 'investments'. DIY investing is a risky activity fraught with pitfalls. Here's a not-so-fun fact: all the research shows that 70%–75% of retail traders lose money. Robinhood and similar apps are designed to make users trade regularly and actively work against the 'invest and forget' approach. They want their clients to trade fast and furiously, even if it means they trade badly.

Investing apps offer easy access to trading, but they encourage impulsive and speculative trading. I see people attracted to highly volatile investments without fully understanding the risks involved. When people have limited investment knowledge or experience, they make uninformed decisions. There's also a danger of the herd mentality where they get caught up in the latest investment trends or 'hot stock'.

Also, many new investors fail to grasp the importance of diversifying across different asset categories. By investing in one sector, they are vulnerable to big losses.

I should add that these apps highlight their commission-free trading, but don't mention hidden fees in currency conversion or account maintenance.

Emotional investing is also a hazard for DIY investors. Let's say an investor has purchased shares of a particular stock at €50 per share, and the market suddenly declines. He is very attached to his hard-earned money. Fear and panic kick in, prompting the investor to immediately sell his shares at €40 per share to avoid further losses.

The investor's decision to sell was driven by fear of losing his money in the market decline rather than a rational assessment of the company's fundamentals or long-term prospects. He lost €10 per share due to a knee-jerk reaction. Chances are that the market will recover soon after and the stock price will rise again. The investor has lost money and is missing out on potential profits.

Having a professional manage your money removes this emotional attachment. You might not want to hear this, but a financial or investment manager looks coolly and dispassionately at their investment portfolio. As a result, they can make a better judgement call on market movements and how to grow your money.

The truth is so-called retail 'investing' is little more than gambling when people fail to educate themselves. Please seek advice from reputable sources before jumping into online trading. If you don't, I suggest only investing what you can afford to lose.

What can I invest in?

You can invest money in many categories of asset. Deciding what's best for you depends on your investment goals, risk tolerance, time horizon and personal preferences. Some assets, such as derivatives, are very complex and come with a lot of risk but potentially very high rewards.

However, let's focus on the basics here. I'll attempt to outline these top investment categories in the coming pages:

- bonds
- property
- stocks, shares and equities
- investment funds (equity, bond, property and index funds)
- commodities
- collectables
- cryptocurrencies (comes with a hazard warning).

Bonds

What are bonds?

Bonds are loans to governments or companies in return for their promise or 'bond' to repay you with interest. In the simplest terms, they are like IOUs.

A government (the bond issuer) gives you (the bondholder) a contractual promise or commitment to repay you with interest. A government bond is sometimes called a gilt.

Governments often use this borrowed money to build roads, hospitals and other 'capital infrastructure'. For example, the National Treasury Management Agency (NTMA) oversees Irish government fundraising. As mentioned above, you can buy Irish government bonds from the NTMA or other authorised financial institutions.

Bonds are a fixed-income investment, providing investors with a predictable and regular income stream. All bonds have a 'fixed term', meaning the loan can range from a few months to several years.

Who should invest in bonds?

The bond market is a strong asset class recommended as part of a diversified investment portfolio. However, it's essential to research and compare bond options before investing.

What are the risks and what are you getting in return?

Bond risk is usually related to the country or company issuing them. Countries with greater economic and political instability are associated with high-risk bonds. These economies have the most attractive yields (higher interest rates) but also a greater chance they may not repay the borrowed money. Some examples of high-risk bonds may include those issued by nations in Africa, South America and certain parts of Asia.

Lower-risk bonds typically come from stable economies, with less likelihood of defaulting on payments. Examples of such countries include the United States, Germany, Japan and the United Kingdom. However, bonds issued by these countries pay low interest rates, and some have even charged people to mind their money for them. This is called a 'negative yield'. Germany began charging investors for bonds in 2014 because of a demand for so-called 'safe-haven' assets.

People like bonds not only for their security but because they have some flexibility. You can buy and sell bonds during a fixed term. If your money is in an Irish ten-year bond, for example, and after five years you need your money back, you can sell it. You sell on something called the bond market. The price that someone pays for your bond will depend on the yield and the term remaining.

Bonds suit those who prefer safer investments or want a steady income stream. They are a tried and trusted method of investing and can be relatively low risk if you lend to a stable entity. They are seen as a reliable option for individuals who want to protect their capital, earn regular interest or diversify their investment portfolio.

Property

Irish people have a fascination with property. Some attribute this obsession to our colonial past. After being dispossessed of our land for generations, we may have had a greater desire to regain ownership and control over land and property.

Property investment became frenzied during the Celtic Tiger years – the nickname for Ireland's economic boom in the late 1990s until 2007. Buying property became a massive symbol of wealth, success and social standing. However, the country's fortunes dramatically reversed in 2008 when the global financial crisis struck. Understandably, people have been far more cautious about investing in property in recent years. The Central Bank also placed tighter restrictions on borrowing levels in 2015. See Section 6: Mortgages for more details on this.

What is property investing?

Property investing involves purchasing a physical property to make a profit, an income or both. As an investment, property is easy to understand. Investors buy a residential or commercial property, hoping the property grows in value each year and beats inflation. This growth in value is called 'capital appreciation'.

Renting out the property gives you an income called 'the yield'.

Rental income from tenants provides a steady cash flow, which helps cover expenses or enables the investor to reinvest in more properties.

A legal lease contract will underpin the rental income you get from a property each year. Leases for residential tenants usually are quite flexible. With a specific notice period, either party can step away. For commercial tenants, they can be a little stricter.

However, property investing is not passive and can be time-consuming and costly. The property must be managed and maintained, and rental agreements must be arranged.

As evidenced by the property crash in Ireland, it can also be a volatile asset. By investing in different properties or many areas, investors can spread their risk and potentially reduce the impact of any one property underperforming.

Who should invest in property?
Property is an asset class best suited for people who already have a large nest egg or savings and want to diversify their portfolio.

Property investing requires a significant upfront investment, at least 30% of the cost of the building as a deposit. Investing in property becomes far riskier when people borrow to buy the asset. The property market can be unpredictable, with prices subject to vast fluctuations.

Supply and demand for property ebbs and flows with the economy. Sometimes, there are more houses on the market than people want, and the prices and values of properties fall. If an investor can't rent the property and the building no longer generates an income, paying back a loan may become difficult or impossible.

There are serious considerations before you borrow to purchase an investment property. It's important to realise that three parties will share the income the property generates: the Revenue Commissioners, the bank and then you.

If you're lucky, the property will produce enough income for the Revenue Commissioners and to repay the bank its mortgage. However, you could wait twenty to twenty-five years until the mortgage ends to receive an income. Property investing is a very long game and is a long-term investment.

Rising interest rates can have a big impact on the cash flow of an investment property. In 2022 and 2023, we experienced dramatic rises in interest rates, which saw many landlords struggle as the cost of their mortgages increased. Often, investors realise too late that they haven't done their figures, and that the income from rent isn't enough to cover the cost of the investment.

Novice investors may also overlook ongoing expenses, such as maintenance, property taxes and insurance. Legislative administration adds to the costs, such as registering with the Residential Tenancies Board. Don't forget the property-management fees if you hire someone to manage the property.

Above all, property is not a passive investment. It takes your time and considerable finances for the upkeep of your investment.

A good property investment also requires knowledge of the local property market and potential rental demand. Successful property investors need patience, awareness and a long-term perspective.

Remember, too, that property is a relatively illiquid asset, as it can often take a few months to years to sell a building.

CLIENT CASE

PAUL, AGED 38

Paul bought an investment property for €500,000 before the 2008 crash. He borrowed €300,000 to buy the property and used €200,000 of his cash savings. I first met him in 2012 when the effects of the crash were still being felt.

The house had lost 50% of its value. He now had an asset worth €250,000, with a loan of €300,000 costing him €1,500 a month in loan repayments. He had difficulty finding good tenants and wasn't making his loan repayments.

It was a mess, but he was one of many. I saw others who invested in commercial property and couldn't find tenants. You can see the rising risk and declining reward. Borrowing to invest in property amplifies that risk. Proceed cautiously if you must borrow to invest in any asset.

How did the Irish property crash happen?

Irish people are more aware than most that property investing is not a guaranteed path to wealth. Anyone around in the late 1990s and early 2000s witnessed the incredible property boom, with prices skyrocketing and a surge in housing construction. Easy access to credit and speculative lending from the banks helped fuel the boom.

Then, Lehman Brothers, an American financial-services firm, collapsed on 15 September 2008, and this precipitated a global financial crisis, which had severe repercussions here. The boom went bust, and property prices began to decline.

Buyers became cautious, leading to an even sharper decrease in property demand, further exacerbating the crash. Property developers and homeowners were trapped in negative equity, where the value of their property fell below the outstanding mortgage amount.

The effects of the property crash in Ireland were far-reaching. They had significant consequences for the construction industry, the banking system and the Irish economy.

While the property crash was a cautionary tale for some, it also presented opportunities for others. Legendary American investor Warren Buffet explains one rule of smart investing: 'We simply attempt to be fearful when others are greedy and to be greedy only when others are fearful.' Some investors with capital went out and snapped up properties at heavily discounted prices and made a lot of money from the crash.

Stocks, shares and equities

For many, the world of stocks, shares and equities seems like a mysterious place populated by high rollers and larger-than-life characters from movies like *The Wolf of Wall Street*. I hope it won't be so mysterious by the end of this section.

What are stocks, shares and equities?

Stocks, shares and equities are tiny pieces of ownership in companies. Think of a company as a giant pie. Then, shares would be slices of the pie (little pieces of a company) and the people who buy these slices of pie are 'shareholders'.

When you buy a few shares in Google, for example, you own a minuscule piece of the company. As a shareholder, you can earn a tiny bit of Google's profits and any growth in value. Your investment may also drop in value if Google shares drop in value.

You can buy shares in a company that is 'publicly traded', which means they have made their shares open to the public to buy on an open market. These shares are traded on stock exchanges. When a company moves from private ownership to being publicly traded, this is known as an Initial Public Offering (IPO).

As more people want the shares because they want to own a part of a company, the share price rises. If there is lower demand, the share price falls.

Share or equity trading is one of the most volatile ways of investing. All the millions of publicly traded companies in every country worldwide will face different levels of supply and demand every day. Good news and bad news emerges about every company every day. The values of shares can fluctuate minute by minute. Because of this volatility, equity investing is one of the riskiest forms of investment. However, the attraction of equity investing is that it has historically provided some of the best returns available of all the asset classes.

Is there a difference between stocks, shares and equities?
Most people use the terms interchangeably, but they have slightly different meanings.

- Shares refer to having ownership in one company. You can tell people, for example, that you own fifty *shares* in Amazon.
- Stock refers to the ownership of shares in multiple companies. You can say, 'I own *stock* in Amazon and Netflix.'
- Equity refers to your ownership stake in any company. Amazon has over 10 billion shares. If you could buy 1 billion of them, you could say, 'I hold a 10% *equity stake* in Amazon.'

Who should invest in stocks and shares?

Investing in individual stocks and shares is high risk. I'd compare it to gambling rather than investing. Many older Irish people know this from bitter experience after the Telecom Éireann shares disaster in 1999. Encouraged by the government, over half a million Irish people bought shares in the newly privatised telecoms company. The shares rose in value at first but tanked within the year. Over 450,000 people who still owned shares lost much of their investment, and it left many who borrowed money to buy the shares in debt.

However, there's a trade-off between risk and returns, and the rewards of investing in shares can also be great. Anyone who was smart enough to invest $1,000 in Apple in the 1980s, when it sold for 11 cents a share, could retire comfortably now, as the shares are worth around $1.6 million.

Despite the risks, some feel it's sexy to have part ownership of a big tech company. Others buy into little-known companies hoping to make fortunes by finding the next big thing or 'hot stock'. Unfortunately, ordinary individuals rarely make millions by stock picking. Those who do are the exception rather than the rule, and the experience of the Telecom Éireann shares disaster is more common.

Investment funds

People often scratch their heads and admit they know nothing about investment funds. It's little wonder, as the financial industry ties up investment funds in so much jargon that it's hard to unravel.

However, they are not really that difficult to understand and, in my experience, investing in regulated investment funds is your safest bet. Even a small monthly investment into the right fund for you will grow and grow if given enough time.

What are investment funds?

Investment funds are best described as big buckets of money (or funds) collected from many people who want to invest. This big bucket of money is used to buy stocks in many companies. Then, firms called 'fund management companies' manage these funds for all the investors.

Investment funds are a safer way to invest in stocks, shares and bonds than buying individual shares yourself. They smooth out the volatility of buying shares or bonds by enabling you to purchase many stocks from lots of companies.

The American investor John Bogle explained the concept of investment funds with the words: 'Don't look for the needle in the haystack. Just buy the haystack!' He meant investors should stop trying to predict the next Apple or Microsoft. Instead, they should buy investment funds, which enable them to put small amounts of money into many stocks.

That way, you don't lose all your money if one company fails. You could still make money if the other companies do very well. With investment funds, you have a greater chance of sharing in the stock market's big market winners.

In Ireland, there are companies like Zurich Life, New Ireland, Standard Life, Aviva Life & Pensions and Irish Life that specialise in these investment funds on behalf of investors. Banks and stockbrokers also offer their own products.

Who should invest in investment funds?

With many categories of investment funds and different risks, there is something suitable for almost everyone to invest in.

Some investment funds offer high-risk, high-return potential, while others are lower risk and lower return options. However, all are similar in attempting to spread the risk by investing in a wide portfolio of stocks and other asset classes.

Ultimately, the risk depends on the investments within each fund and broader market conditions.

What types of investment funds can I buy?

These are the primary funds that Irish people invest in:

- equity funds
- index fund
- bond funds
- property funds
- exchange-traded funds (ETFs)

What are equity funds?

In an equity fund, you put your money together with other people, and a fund manager takes care of buying stocks and shares from many companies.

Fund managers may choose to focus on specific baskets of stocks and companies. For example, you can invest in a technology equity fund with a diversified portfolio of stocks, such as Apple, Microsoft, Amazon and Facebook. You could also invest in a 'sustainable fund' which contains stock from companies that are focused on positively impacting the environment or society.

Who should buy equity funds?

As equity funds are primarily invested in stocks, they are long-term investments. They can be suitable for investors with a higher risk tolerance and a long-term investment horizon. Consider equity funds if you are comfortable with the volatility of stocks and can invest over a long duration.

What are index funds?

These funds often follow a stock index of companies, like the Dow Jones or the FTSE 100. They buy some of all the stocks in that index, which helps to spread the risk.

What is a stock index?

Each stock index is made up of different companies, like a team of companies.

- The Dow Jones index, for example, comprises thirty companies, including Apple, Microsoft, Disney and Coca-Cola. These companies are leaders in American industries.

- The FTSE 100 index represents the hundred largest companies on the London Stock Exchange.
- The S&P 500 index is a big club that includes five hundred of the most influential companies in the United States. These companies come from different industries, like technology, finance and retail.
- Other popular indices (plural for index) include the Nikkei 225 in Japan and the DAX in Germany.

Each stock index tracks and measures the performance of a group of selected stocks listed on the stock exchanges worldwide. They calculate an overall score using the sales performance of shares in their companies. As a result, each index gives us an idea of how well the stock market is doing, and their results work like report cards for economies.

When people buy many stocks from these companies, stock prices on the indices go up. If people are selling stocks, the prices go down. The Dow Jones, for example, is an important marker for the overall health of the American economy. The ISEQ index is like a scorecard for how well companies in Ireland are doing in the stock market.

Who should buy index funds?

As they offer broad market exposure, they can be a good choice for investors seeking a more passive approach to investing. Index funds are typically lower in cost and can be suitable for investors focused on the long term while maintaining a diversified portfolio.

What are bond funds?

As discussed earlier, a bond is a loan to a government or big company that needs to borrow money. Each government or company gives their 'bond' to pay back the money with interest.

A bond fund is slightly different to a bond. If you invest in a bond fund, you put your money together with other people's money into a fund that invests in hundreds of different bonds. A fund manager controls the fund and takes care of all the lending.

Who should buy bond funds?

Bond funds can be suitable for investors with a lower tolerance for risk. They can offer lower but steadier forms of income and are generally considered less volatile than equity funds. Investing in a bond fund may also be less risky than individual bonds.

A bond fund holds hundreds of different bonds from many nations rather than having bonds of an individual issuer. If a single country goes into default or cannot repay its bond debts, there is less risk to your investment.

Bond funds can be suitable for investors seeking a safe and steady – if lower – return for their capital.

What are property funds?

When you invest in a property fund, you combine your money with other people's money, and a fund manager chooses a basket of properties in which to invest. These property assets can include everything from shopping centres, industrial estates and offices to residential houses and apartments. As an investor in property funds, you own a small part of these properties and earn a share of the rental income and any capital appreciation.

Who should buy property funds?

Property funds can be an attractive alternative for those seeking to invest in property without the hassle of buying individual properties.

These funds offer income generation through rental payments and asset appreciation, so they suit investors seeking a mix of incomes. Different funds contain various properties in many markets, offering mixed investment risks – many are high risk.

What are exchange-traded funds?

Exchange-traded funds (ETFs) are like a virtual basket of assets. A single ETF can contain dozens or hundreds of stocks, bonds or anything considered an investable asset.

Some ETFs are index funds that aim to track an index – like the S&P 500 – and require less active management. Others focus on bonds or commodities, for example, and others are a mix of everything.

ETFs and equity funds are similar in enabling investors to access baskets of company shares. However, ETFs trade on stock exchanges like individual stocks, meaning they are bought or sold throughout the trading day at market prices. Equity funds do not trade on the stock exchange.

ETFs are also passively managed and aim to replicate the returns of the index.

Who should buy ETFs?

Because ETFs have less active management, they often have lower management fees than actively managed funds. This makes ETFs attractive to some investors. ETFs offer flexibility in trading and suit investors who prefer more active trading or want exposure to specific sectors or asset classes. However, many Irish investors are discouraged from investing in them because of the high taxes on ETF profits in Ireland. As with all complex investments, speak to a financial professional for advice.

Commodities

What are commodities?

Commodities are things that people need and use every day, like oil, gold or coffee. They are often raw materials (primary goods) that are used in the production of goods and services. They include crude oil, natural gas, metals (gold, silver, copper), agricultural products (wheat, corn, soybeans) and livestock (cattle, pigs).

How do I invest in commodities?

Direct investment

You can buy physical commodities, such as gold bullion or silver coins, and store them yourself.

Futures contracts

Futures contracts are agreements to buy or sell commodities at a specific price and date in the future. They are traded on exchanges and enable investors to speculate on the price movements of commodities without holding the physical assets. However, futures contracts require a high level of understanding and are best bought and sold by experienced traders.

Investment funds

We've discussed investment funds above. Professional fund managers pool money from multiple people to invest in commodities. Investment funds probably offer the easiest way for the average person to invest in commodities.

Collectables

What are collectables?

Besides the traditional asset classes, some investors venture into prestige investments, such as art, wine, cars or antiques.

Who should invest in collectables?

Many luxury collectables are vanity investments for the rich and super-rich. At the very least, an investor in collectables must be a specialist in the field or have access to trustworthy specialists.

These classes of investments can offer great returns but require extensive knowledge or professional advice. They are also risky investments – art, antiques and cars can suffer from the vagaries of fashion. What is fashionable and in demand in the mid-2020s may not be by the mid-2030s.

Collectables are also called 'illiquid' assets – they are difficult to convert into cash. They are more long-term investments, sometimes decades long.

Cryptocurrencies

What are cryptocurrencies?

When we talk about investing in cryptocurrency, we're referring to buying digital money that only exists online. Just like we use physical money to buy things, cryptocurrency is virtual money used to make online transactions. People worldwide use these virtual coins to trade for goods and services. Bitcoin and Ethereum are two examples of collections of cryptocurrencies.

Unlike physical money, cryptocurrency works on something called 'blockchain' technology. This means that whenever a transaction occurs, it gets recorded on a digital public ledger called a blockchain. This helps to keep track of who owns which coins.

Those who invest in cryptocurrency bet that these virtual coins' values will increase over time. Some people invest in cryptocurrency because they believe it is the future of money and its value will keep growing. People are attracted to investing in it because of the potential for high returns. However, cryptocurrency is an extremely volatile investment, making it high risk.

Who should invest in cryptocurrencies?

In short, only those with a huge risk tolerance for losing money should invest in cryptocurrencies. Very few professional investors have the depth of knowledge to navigate that virtual world of finance. It's hard to use and harder to understand.

I've seen many people left financially bereft because they invested in non-regulated products over the years. Investors of cryptocurrencies remind me of those who invested in off-the-plan Bulgarian properties that were never built because of the global crash in 2008.

I'll give my last word on cryptocurrencies to the legendary investor Warren Buffet: 'Stay away from it. It's a mirage, basically. In terms of cryptocurrencies, generally, I can say almost with certainty that they will come to a bad ending.'

What is the financial planner's role in investing?

Firstly, I'll tell you what it's not. My day-to-day role, and that of my colleagues, is not to be that person who sits in front of nine screens, analysing vast banks of market data.

When it comes to my own money, I don't invest in individual stocks. I have a fund manager who invests in investment funds for me. Although I have experience, education and knowledge of investment markets, I'm also a busy business owner. I'm the CEO and a shareholder in several companies. I have a wife and four kids. I don't have time to sit at my laptop trying to figure out investment markets. I pay the experts to do it for me. And there's nothing wrong with that. There is so much bad content online saying people should track this index and do that, and it's all nonsense.

All the above information about stocks, shares and investment funds is an excellent introduction to investing. However, you need decades of experience to have real insight into this area.

As a financial planner, I need a good working knowledge of the markets and an understanding of the asset classes and available products. Then, I match them to my client's financial goals. But I'm not a 'stock picker', trying to beat the market by finding the next 'hot stock' or share in a 'hot' new company. If you ever encounter someone who advises you to invest in an individual share, please run a million miles. It's like putting your money on a horse at the bookies.

I leave stock picking to Warren Buffet, one of the world's greatest and most experienced investors. And I leave managing funds to the best fund managers. That's their niche, their expertise.

My job is to assess a client's needs and financial goals first and then find the best path for them through the investment maze. I need a bird's-eye view of a client's finances to spot the gaps in their plans and remedy them. Then, I seek out some of the best funds and fund managers. I find the investment funds that will suit the client's goals, but I leave the fund management to those who work on the coalface of the investment markets. They're the experts.

What's the simplest way to invest?

I've given you the basics to be a DIY investor. You can sit down and do months and months of research on millions of funds and bonds out there. And this is great if you have the time and interest. Tread cautiously but go for it. However, if you want to avoid the stress and headaches, you can do what I do and let the experts do it for you.

For example, I have an askpaul investment fund that I set up during COVID-19. More than 3,500 have signed up, and over 3,000 follow the fund I use. I started investing €500 a month and now invest €2,000 a month. But I don't manage the fund. I examined the fund, saw that it was right for me and then let the fund manager take over. They charge me an annual management fee to do this. It's worth it because the fund has an average of a 10% return over the past thirty-three years. I don't make it complicated. I pay experts to manage that fund for me.

Similarly, when people come to me and want to invest, I make a plan and present them with the best fund options. 'Here's the fund. Here's how it works. This is why I believe this fund will work best for you.' It doesn't have to be complicated if you're willing to take advice from an expert.

Yes, please read all the details of the asset classes I've detailed above. Make sure you have a good grounding in the subject before you invest. To be a good investor, you need to make *informed* decisions. But to be *fully* informed, you still need to look for expert advice. That's what I do.

Quiz

What should I invest in?

- What is your investment goal? What is your 'why'? Why do you want to invest?
- What is your risk tolerance? Can you afford to lose some of this money?
- What is your time horizon? How long can you keep this money invested? Can you wait if it drops in value?
- What sort of investment appeals to you? What are your personal preferences?

Consider these questions and armed with the answers, consult a financial specialist to find the right investment for you.

CLIENT CASE

ANNA, AGED 25

Anna is an entrepreneur who launched a health, beauty and fitness business. The business has enjoyed enormous success and Anna has amassed substantial cash reserves in a few years.

She came to us because she struggled to know what to do with all this money sitting in a company business account. She received investment suggestions from people who I call 'bar-stool advisors'. They told her to take the money out of the business, pay tax on it and buy a house worth €1 million in France.

Luckily, she went for professional advice first. Anna didn't know where she wanted to live or what she wanted to do in a year. So why, at age twenty-five, would she want to be shackled to a €1 million house in Spain?

Despite all her success in her industry, she felt overwhelmed by having all that money.

We have just finished a financial plan where she has an excellent pension and investment account set up through her limited company. This has given her peace of mind. Anna's biggest headache over the past year was overthinking what to do with the money in her business. Sometimes, wealth can bring its own problems. With the money now working for Anna, that stress has been removed.

She can focus on making a great business even more successful, knowing that her wealth and future are secure. The way she's going, she'll be able to retire by thirty-five if that's what she wants.

Will Anna's financial plan always look the way it is now? No, because Anna's personal and business life will change in the coming years. That's why the financial plan needs to have flexibility and regular reviews.

CLIENT CASE

MARK & ANNE, AGED 43 & 41

This couple had €1.5 million in bank deposits and investments – a huge amount of savings. They interviewed a few financial planners but picked us as their planners, which was an excellent win for our business.

The deposit rates with banks were negligible. And their investment opportunities were with 'tied agents' or third parties with high commissions and fees. We moved their investment accounts to similar ones with a much-reduced charging structure. That move alone has put a projected extra €200,000 into their investment fund when it matures.

Of course, you don't need to invest €1 million to see a financial planner. Whatever you're investing, it's worth seeking advice – otherwise, the financial hit to you can be huge. Banks and other firms will reap the benefits of your money if you pay a lot of commissions and fees.

Your 7-point action plan for saving and investing

- Are you ready to invest? Complete the quiz on p108–9.
- Know why you should invest.
- Understand the different asset classes.
- Understand the basics of investment funds.
- What assets should you invest in? Complete the quiz on p145.
- Understand the pitfalls of 'retail investing' and cryptocurrencies.
- Actively seek a reputable and impartial financial planner to partner with you when you're ready to invest.

SECTION 4
TAX

The first time the taxman entered my life, I was seven years old. I was in religion class at St Mary's National School in Tallaght and the teacher was reading about Matthew in the Bible and how he became one of the twelve apostles.

Passing along, Jesus saw a man at his work collecting taxes. His name was Matthew. Jesus said, 'Come along with me.' Matthew stood up and followed him.

The teacher read on and we heard that the Pharisees, or holy men, considered it scandalous that Jesus hung around with Matthew.

A classmate piped up. 'But why, sir? Why did they not like Matthew?'

The teacher replied with a laugh, 'No one likes the taxman!'

I'd also heard about the taxman in those long business chats my father and brother-in-law, David, had around the kitchen table at night. I couldn't wait to talk to my dad when he got home. After ten hours working on a building site, I'm sure it was exactly what he needed.

'What's the story about the taxman, Dad? My teacher says no one likes the taxman.'

I can't remember my dad's expression or tone, but I'll never forget what he said, 'Your teacher forgot those taxes pay his wages.'

So, I grew up believing that taxes were fair and necessary.

When I was fifteen, I started working as a lounge boy in The Spawell in Templeogue. After my first weekend, the floor manager handed me a small brown envelope containing my payslip and some cash. I immediately counted the money and thought she'd short-changed me. When I challenged her, she reacted like my teacher had all those years ago. 'No one likes the taxman, kid.'

Once again, I consulted with my dad at home. I assumed taxes were for adults earning a full-time wage. Surely, as a fifteen-year-old working part-time, I didn't have to pay taxes? However, Dad quickly re-educated me. In short, yes, I had to pay tax. We all contribute to the system. I was outraged.

All these years later, aged forty-one, I still have conflicting feelings about tax. I understand that raising taxes for government expenditure is necessary, but I don't always agree with how it's collected – or spent.

I have a friend who regularly emails the TDs in his constituency. He lets them know his opinion about everything – from changes in the budget to the spiralling costs of the new children's hospital project. He's a self-employed businessman with eight employees, all paying their taxes, and he believes in having a say in how those taxes are spent.

Even if his emails are largely ignored, my friend understands taxes matter. Your taxes matter.

You should care about them and how they are spent. You must also understand the system – or, potentially, you may pay more than you need to.

This book aims to increase your overall financial knowledge, and taxation is a core part of personal budgeting. A good working knowledge of the tax system is crucial, regardless of your income level, as it directly impacts your finances and financial goals.

In this section, I'll explain the Irish tax system and how it impacts your income. I will also discuss the taxes that might affect you as your lifecycle evolves. Armed with a greater knowledge of taxation, you can reduce tax liabilities, maximise your income and increase your financial health.

What is tax?

Tax is a compulsory financial charge imposed on all of us by our government to generate revenue to fund public services and responsibilities. Taxes pay for all state- or public-sector employees, including nurses and other healthcare workers, school teachers, members of An Garda Síochána, the defence forces, firefighters, judges, politicians and civil servants.

It also pays for hospitals, schools, roads and transport. Taxes fund pensions and social-welfare payments for those unable to work or find work.

Who collects tax?

The Irish government agency responsible for customs, excise, taxation and related matters is the Revenue Commissioners, though it's commonly called Revenue.

A seventeenth-century French finance minister called Jean Baptiste Colbert best described the taxman's job: 'The art of taxation consists in so plucking the goose as to obtain the largest possible amount of feathers with the smallest possible amount of hissing.'

Who pays tax?

Everybody pays tax in one form or another. Even the child who buys a small bar of chocolate in the corner shop with his pocket money pays 23% VAT on his sweets.

How is tax collected?

The main ways Revenue collects taxes are through payroll, direct debits or self-assessment filings from self-employed workers.

Employers collect taxes from employees on behalf of the Revenue via Pay As You Earn. Self-employed people pay self-assessment at the end of the tax year. Businesses charge and collect Revenue's consumer tax, known as VAT, whenever someone buys goods or services.

What are the main tax categories in Ireland?

- **Income tax:** Everyone earning above a certain income pays income tax. This includes income from employment, self-employment, most social-welfare payments, rental income, and savings and investments.

- **Pay As You Earn (PAYE)**: This method of tax collection is the responsibility of employers. They must deduct all income tax and social insurance from employees' wages or occupational pension before paying their net wages or pension. The PAYE system incorporates income tax, the Universal Social Charge (USC) and Pay Related Social Insurance (PRSI), which provides social-welfare benefits.

- **Universal Social Charge (USC)**: This form of income tax applies to everyone with income over a certain threshold. It is separate and distinct from income tax and PRSI and was introduced in 2011 as part of the government's emergency measures during the 2008 financial crisis. USC is payable on gross income.

- **Corporation tax**: Companies that are resident in Ireland and non-resident companies that carry on a trade in Ireland pay this tax. The controversial issue of multinational corporations and their tax practices often surfaces in the news. Ireland's low corporate tax rate draws both praise and criticism.

- **Value Added Tax (VAT)**: This 'consumption' tax is already included in the price of most goods and services. Businesses selling goods or services are responsible for collecting this tax but, ultimately, it is us consumers who pay it.

- **Local Property Tax (LPT)**: Owners of residential property pay LPT. It doesn't matter if the owner lives abroad – if they own residential property in Ireland, they owe this tax.

- **Capital Gains Tax (CGT)**: When we dispose of (sell) assets and make a profit from the sale, we pay CGT. The tax is on the profit or gain.
- **Capital Acquisitions Tax (CAT)**: This tax is paid on gifts and inheritances. You may receive gifts and inheritances up to a set value over your lifetime before paying CAT.
- **Excise duty**: This refers to a charge on goods, such as alcohol and tobacco, petrol and diesel.
- **Customs duty**: These are tariffs on goods transported into Ireland.
- **Vehicle Registration Tax (VRT)**: This applies to every car registered in Ireland.
- **Stamp duty**: This tax is charged on the transfer of property – all buildings, land and homes in Ireland. It also applies to bank cards and credit cards. It is applied to levies on insurance premiums, pensions and the transfer of stocks and shares.

How does politics influence tax?

Ireland has experienced little of the political polarisation that has been seen in the UK, the US, Brazil and some countries in Central Europe, where there are wild swings between people on the left and right of the political spectrum.

Conservatives and those on the right promote capitalism and advocate for lower taxes. They believe capitalism and lower taxes spur economic growth and encourage entrepreneurship and wealth creation. Socialists and those on the left believe in more equitable wealth distribution and generally advocate for higher taxes to be levied on higher incomes. They believe the government's role is to redistribute wealth to address social inequalities.

Throughout a century of independent rule, Ireland's politics has been immune to big swings between right and left, and so has its taxation policies. Essentially, we are a nation of the middle. We're moderates who gently sway between centre left, centre or centre right.

We know we should pay taxes but don't want to pay too much. We want a social-welfare safety net but don't want it to be too generous. This may change should Sinn Féin or a socialist-leaning coalition head a government.

When do I need a tax advisor?

I'd like to explain tax in jargon-free, plain English. However, there is no plain English when it comes to taxation. The conspiracy theorist in me could believe the system was designed to overwhelm and confuse us so much that no one questions it any more. In reality, our tax system is Frankenstein's monster – made of bolted-on legislation, last-minute amendments and constantly changing design.

Self-employed people should have a bookkeeper or an accountant to do their tax returns. For business owners, of course, a tax advisor is a must.

As a result, much of the focus in this section will be on PAYE workers.

However, I highly recommend getting a tax advisor to assist you in most dealings with the Revenue Commissioners. Having a tax advisor may sound excessive and expensive, but there are good online tax companies with a pay-if-you-win type service. If you have any doubts about your tax returns, I recommend a tax advisor because:

- You don't want to risk making an error. This can be expensive after Revenue adds interest, taxes and charges.
- You don't have the time or energy to wade through section and verse of various tax schedules.

How much tax is collected in Ireland?

In 2022, the Revenue Commissioners collected a total of €82.2 billion.

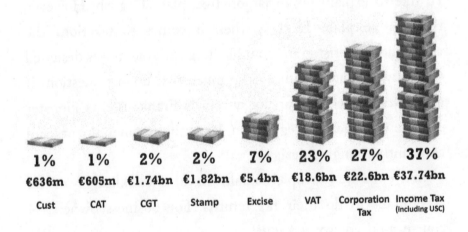

TAX RECEIPTS

1%	1%	2%	2%	7%	23%	27%	37%
€636m	€605m	€1.74bn	€1.82bn	€5.4bn	€18.6bn	€22.6bn	€37.74bn
Cust	CAT	CGT	Stamp	Excise	VAT	Corporation Tax	Income Tax (including USC)

What taxes do I need to know about?

For this book, I'm going to focus on the four main areas that affect personal budgeting, income and investments:

- Income tax, PAYE and USC
- Capital Gains Tax
- Capital Acquisitions Tax
- Other taxes: Exit taxes on investments and DIRT on savings.

Many additional taxes, like VAT, excise duty and corporation tax, fall into the sphere of business tax.

Income tax

What is income tax?

The primary source of taxes for the Revenue Commissioners comes from income tax. In 2022, €37.7 billion or 37% of total revenue came from income taxes paid by you, me and everyone else in this country who is paid a wage.

Income tax is the tax imposed on the income earned by everyone, including employees, self-employed people and business owners. It is a direct tax levied by the Irish government on the income generated within the country.

Irish income tax is progressive, meaning the tax rate increases as the income level rises. The tax rates and bands are subject to change each year and are set out in the annual budget.

What income tax will I pay?

In this section, I aim to give you a practical and straightforward insight into an overly complicated system. What we don't understand, we fear – and what we fear, we avoid. There is nothing to fear in this space.

Your tax bill will depend on:

- Your income
- The income tax band you fall into
- Other taxes and levies
- The income tax credits you are allowed
- Income tax allowances and expenses.

What income is taxed?

Income tax is charged on all income. That includes wages, salaries, profits and pension payments. Income tax can extend to any company perks, such as a company car or health insurance. People often forget that tax is payable on bonus payments, commissions and overtime.

People earn income in different ways. Most people reading this book will receive income from one, two or all four categories:

- Employed people get a salary from working for someone.
- Self-employed people work for themselves as sole traders or in a limited company. They can also hire themselves out as a contract worker.
- Investment income, dividend income or rental income are sources of earnings for some people.
- Social-welfare payments and the state pension is a primary source of income for many.

The one thing that all these categories of income have in common is that they are all subject to income tax, PRSI, USC and other levies.

What are the income tax bands?

The amount you earn dictates the percentage of tax you are charged. In Ireland, we have two rates of income tax: 20% and 40%. When we talk about the standard rate of tax, we're referring to the 20% tax bracket. Any income above the standard rate is taxed at the higher rate of 40%.

The table on tax bands below is the starting point for everyone. You calculate your total income for the year, then determine what tax band you lie in.

Your salary may lie entirely in the 20% tax band. However, when you earn more than the 20% tax band limit, the balance of your earnings is taxed at 40%.

PERSONAL CIRCUMSTANCES	2023 (€)	2024 (€)
Single or widowed or surviving civil partner, without qualifying child	40,000 @ 20% Balance @ 40%	42,000 @ 20% Balance @ 40%
Single or widowed or surviving civil partner, qualifying for single person child carer credit	44,000 @ 20% Balance @ 40%	46,000 @ 20% Balance @40%
Married or in a civil partnership, one spouse or civil partner with income	49,000 @ 20% Balance @ 40%	51,000 @ 20% Balance @ 40%
Married or in a civil partnership, both spouses or civil partners with income	49,000 @ 20% with increase of 31,000 Balance @ 40%	51,000 @ 20% with increase of 33,000 Balance @ 40%

Single people and how the tax bands work

Joe and Hugh are brothers. Joe is single and, in 2024, has a salary of €42,000. His entire income is taxed at 20%, the lower (or standard) rate of income tax.

Hugh is also single but earns €50,000 in 2024. The first €42,000 of his earnings are taxed at the 20% standard rate. The balance of Hugh's earnings – €8,000 – is taxed at the higher rate of 40%.

Moving up the tax bands

Ideally, you want to break into that upper tax bracket as you advance in your working life. This is an advantage when building a pension and getting tax relief at the 40% rate. (More about this in Section 7 (Pensions).)

Please also dismiss bar-stool advice, telling you not to go for promotion or work overtime as 'you're only paying more tax'. This is just plain silly. Yes, the more you earn, the more tax you pay – but you also make more money and have more in your bank account.

If you earn €38,000 and are lucky enough to get a €10,000 increase, you will pay 40% income tax on some of that increase. But you don't pay the higher tax of 40% on all your income. It only applies to whatever income you earn over the standard tax rate. So, in this example, you will only pay 40% on €6,000.

The point is, be very careful about taking advice from people who simply don't know what they're talking about. Refusing the opportunity to earn more income because there may be more tax to pay baffles me. Receiving an increase in your salary is always a positive thing.

Married or in a civil partnership and the tax bands

In 2024, the standard rate cut-off point for a married couple or civil partners is €51,000. If both are working, this standard cut-off point is increased by the lower of:

- the income of the lower earner

OR

- €33,000

Let's use a married couple, Charlie and Jerry, as an example.

Charlie, who earns more than Jerry, pays at the 20% tax rate up to the cut-off for a married couple – €51,000 of his earnings. Jerry makes less and has the standard tax rate applied to the first €33,000 in earnings.

Both incomes add up to €84,000.

Remember, if the couple are unmarried, they can earn up to €42,000 each or €84,000 in total on the lower rate.

The only advantage for married or civil partners lies when they are in separate tax bands, so one in 20% and the other in 40%.

A married couple's advantage in the tax bands

Let's compare the tax bands for Charlie and Jerry as single people and after they get married. Charlie has an income of €60,000 and Jerry's is €35,000. Charlie is in the 40% tax band and Jerry is in the 20% rate.

	SINGLE LIFE	MARRIED LIFE
Income: Charlie	**€60,000**	**€60,000**
Tax @ 20%	€42,000	€51,000
Tax @ 40%	€18,000	€9,000
Income: Jerry	**€35,000**	**€35,000**
Tax @ 20%	€35,000	€33,000
Tax @ 40%	€00,000	€2,000

Before they marry, the couple have €18,000 taxed at 40%. After they marry, they only have €11,000 taxed at the higher rate. In this example, they could save €7,000 at 20% if they marry – which means a tax saving of €1,400 per year.

So, if you consider popping the question, do it for love, not tax reasons. The potential savings aren't much, especially when you factor in the wedding cost – five figures and counting …

CLIENT CASE
LEE & SARAH, AGED 28

Lee and Sarah were married on 1 July 2023, and continued to be taxed as single people until the end of the tax year on 31 December.

However, they are due a refund if they paid more tax as two single people than they would have done if they had been jointly assessed from the date of marriage to the year end. This refund can only be claimed after 31 December of the year of marriage.

As single people, Lee and Sarah paid €10,640 in income tax for the year. Lee paid €9,140 and Sarah paid €1,500. If they had been jointly assessed, they would have paid €8,840.

The difference is €1,800 – as they were married six months, they are due a refund of €900 (€1,800 * 6/12) in 2024.

CLIENT CASE

MICHAEL & JOANNA, AGED 40 & 38

Michael and Joanna are a married couple taxed in the higher tax bracket. Michael earns €60,000 and Joanna earns €44,000.

Joanna is expecting a child in June 2024, so she will be taking maternity leave and her income will decrease. She will earn €22,000 from her job and an additional €6,812 in maternity benefit from her PRSI contributions. Both sources of income are taxable.

As a result, her gross income for 2024 will be €28,812. This means she can transfer an extra €9,000 to her spouse (to bring him up to the cut-off point for a married couple), which will be taxed at 20%.

Michael:
€51,000 @ 20%
€9,000 @ 40%

Joanna

€28,812 @ 20%

If Joanna stays on unpaid leave for another six months, her income will decrease to €22,000 in 2025, so she can transfer over €9,000 to Michael.

What other taxes on income do we pay?

The Universal Social Charge

The Universal Social Charge (USC) is the first tax applied to your income. It's charged on your gross income before deductions, such as pension contributions or PRSI, are taken out.

- The first €25,750 of your income is charged at a 2% rate.
- Income between €25,750 and €70,044 is charged at a 4% rate.
- Income over €70,044 is charged at an 8% rate.

Tax credits or tax relief (except for certain capital allowances) will not reduce the amount of USC you must pay.

Pay Related Social Insurance

Pay Related Social Insurance (PRSI) is a tax that is paid by all employees, whether full-time or part-time, with earnings of €38 or more per week. Self-employed workers with an income of €5,000 a year or more also pay PRSI. The calculations for PRSI are complicated, but the amount you pay will depend on your earnings and the social-insurance class you are insured under.

What are income tax credits?

Everyone has 'tax credits', which give us reductions on our tax bill. The number of tax credits you receive per year is based on your circumstances, and it's possible to use multiple credits at one time.

Some common tax credits include:
- The single personal tax credit, which is worth €1,875
- The employee, or PAYE, tax credit is available to those subject to PAYE deductions and is worth €1,875.
- The earned income credit is open to the self-employed or those in a trade or profession and is also worth €1,875.

Below is the list of some of the primary tax credits.

PERSONAL CIRCUMSTANCES	2023 (€)	2024 (€)
Single person	1,775	**1,875**
Married or in a civil partnership	3,550	**3,750**
Employee Tax Credit	1,775	**1,875**
Widowed person or surviving civil partner (without qualifying child)	1,775	**1,875**
Single person Child Carer Tax Credit	1,650	**1,750**
Incapacitated Child Credit	3,300	**3,500**
Blind Tax Credit Single person	1,650	1,650
Married or in a civil partnership		
• one spouse or civil partner blind	1,650	1,650
• both spouses or civil partners blind	3,300	3,300
Widowed Parent		
• Bereaved in 2023	0,000	3,600
• Bereaved in 2022	3,600	3,150
• Bereaved in 2021	3,150	2,700
• Bereaved in 2020	2,700	2,250
• Bereaved in 2019	2,250	1,800

PERSONAL CIRCUMSTANCES	2023 (€)	2024 (€)
Age Tax Credit		
• Single or widowed or surviving civil partner	1,650	1,650
• Married or in a civil partnership	3,300	3,300
Dependant Relative	245	245
Home Carer Tax Credit	1,700	**1,800**

You can claim the yearly Age Tax Credit if you are sixty-five years or older in the tax year, or are jointly assessed or separately assessed and your partner is sixty-five years or older in the tax year. More credits are available for those with disabilities – you can find the complete list on www.revenue.ie.

Please note that tax credits are only applied after your tax has been calculated.

How do tax credits work?

Ivanna is a single woman earning €40,000. She is taxed at the standard rate of 20%, which means her tax bill is €8,000.

She receives the 'single person tax credit' of €1,875, so Revenue reduces her tax bill to €6,125.

However, Ivanna is also a PAYE worker who is entitled to the 'employee tax credit' of €1,875.

This reduces her tax bill further to €4,250.

What is an income tax allowance?

Tax allowances, or tax reliefs, are another way to reduce your tax bill. The allowance is deducted from your income before tax is calculated.

Pension payments are an excellent example of a tax allowance. Allowances are also available for medical- and dental-insurance premiums, medical expenses, nursing-home expenses, etc. The complete list of tax allowances and reliefs can be found on www. revenue.ie.

Tax was one of the most challenging modules of my CFP® exams, so I know any good financial planner can work with you to minimise taxes. Not evade taxes, minimise them.

Tax allowance from a pension contribution

Jerry earns an income of €58,000 and makes a pension contribution of €5,000. The calculation for tax is: €58,000 − €5,000 = €53,000. Jerry has reduced his taxable income by €5,000, so he has saved 40% of €5,000, which is €2,000.

Every person who pays income tax should consider starting a pension so their pension contributions can reduce the tax they pay. (I discuss this in greater depth in Section 7 (Pensions).)
If you have a tax liability from earned income, you can reduce it substantially by making a pension contribution. Unfortunately, many people don't realise that reducing this tax liability is also open to PAYE workers, not just the self-employed.

In the finance world, we know the months of October to November as 'pension season'. The reason? Self-employed individuals must pay their income tax by the 31 October deadline, or by 15 November if they are submitting their returns online.

CLIENT CASE
COLM, AGED 45

Colm is a PAYE worker. In 2023, he earned €80,000, so €40,000 of his salary is taxable at the 40% rate.

We looked at Colm's company pension. He has a pension in which he and his employer contribute 5% of his gross salary each. They each pay €4,000 a year or a 10% contribution of €8,000.

Revenue has an annual limit for pension tax allowances based on age. (See details in Section 7 (Pensions).)

Being forty-five years old, the maximum tax allowance for Colm is 25% of his €80,000 salary – or €20,000. This means Colm can still make a pension contribution of €16,000 before 31 October 2024 (€20,000 income minus €4,000 from his 5% company pension contribution).

As a result, Colm can receive tax relief of 40% on €16,000, which amounts to €6,400. So, Revenue will return €6,400 from his income tax to fund Colm's pension instead of the national coffers.

A lot of people wrongly believe their maximum pension contribution includes their employer's contribution. In the above example, Colm boosts his pension by 30% of his salary – 25% from him and 5% from his employer.

What is a tax credit certificate?

Your tax credit certificate (TCC) shows the rate of tax that applies to your income and the tax credits you're entitled to. It sets out the following details for the tax year:

- Tax credits, reliefs and rate band
- Universal Social Charge rates and rate band
- Employment Identifier, a unique reference set by your employer for your employment.

You can view, print or download your TCC through the MyAccount facility on Revenue's website to make sure it's correct and up to date.

Revenue will automatically issue you a new tax credit certificate at the start of the tax year, and they give employers a revenue payroll notification (RPN) to deduct the correct amount of tax. Your TCC and RPN instruct your employer on calculating the tax you owe. Revenue also updates your TCC and RPN if your circumstances change during the year.

What about business owners and taxes?

I'd need another book dedicated to this subject to cover company tax structures and how to reap the benefits for building wealth.

If you're a business owner and making profits, you have an advantage over PAYE workers. You can make your profit work harder for you in a limited company. Below are a few notes for limited company owners.

- Profit is taxed at 12.5% on trading income or 25% for non-trading income. An example of a non-trading income is profits from an investment company.

- Company owners can place more funds into a company pension plan (avoiding 12.5% corporate tax).
- You can use Entrepreneurs Relief when you are selling or liquidating your business. Capital Gains Tax reduces from 33% to 10% on the first €1,000,000.
- From the age of fifty-five, you may be able to use Retirement Relief to take up to €750,000 tax-free from your business.
- You can structure your business so that a holding company holds your business shares. Profits can go to the holding company without leaking tax to Revenue. If you take cash from the holding company, it will be subject to tax. However, this strategy allows you to defer tax and use the capital and money to invest and grow your company.

What are allowable expenses for running a business?

- Accountancy fees
- Employees' pay
- Interest payment against business loans
- Buying goods for resale (stock, for example)
- Rent
- Bills for running the business (heat, electricity, broadband, phone, etc.)
- Leasing of vehicles or machinery

You must determine how much of the expenditure is for business purposes and claim a deduction only for that amount. If running a business from home, for example, you should calculate how much heat, electricity and phone bills are for personal or business use.

You may also claim for certain expense before setting up your business, e.g. business plans, professional advice, advertising cost.

Capital Acquisitions Tax

What is Capital Acquisitions Tax?

Capital Acquisitions Tax (CAT) is also known as gift or inheritance tax. This is a tax on capital – cash, property, investments – you acquire or inherit. Sometimes, you can plan to acquire or be gifted these funds. Other times, you can't. A spouse or civil partner is exempt from CAT.

How much CAT do I pay?

The amount of tax you pay depends on the amount of the gift or inheritance from the disponer – 'disponer' is a legal term for the person who provided the gift or inheritance.

The amount you pay also depends on your relationship with the disponer as laid out in Groups A, B and C.

- **Group A**: Children and foster children of the disponer. This group is allowed a tax-free lifetime threshold of €335,000 on gifts and inheritances before CAT is applied.
- **Group B**: Parents, siblings, nieces, nephews, a civil partner's children, grandparents and grandchildren of the disponer. Before CAT applies, they are allowed a tax-free threshold of €32,500 on gifts and inheritances.
- **Group C**: Everyone else – this group is allowed a tax-free threshold of €16,250 on gifts or inheritances before CAT is applied.

These tax-free gifts or inheritances thresholds are spread over a lifetime. For example, if in 2023 you received €100,000 from one of your parents, your Group A tax-free threshold for any future gifts or inheritances would reduce from €335,000 to €235,000. The standard rate of CAT for gifts and inheritances after the tax-free threshold is 33%.

> ## CLIENT CASE
> ## CAROLINE, AGED 49
> Caroline inherited €500,000 from her father in 2023. This meant she fell under Group A in CAT thresholds so could receive €335,000 tax free. Her inheritance of €500,000 minus her tax-free threshold of €335,000 equalled to a taxable inheritance of €165,000. This was taxed at 33 %, so the total inheritance tax Caroline had to pay was €54,450.

What is a CAT-exempt 'gift'?
You may receive a gift up to the value of €3,000 from any person in any calendar year without paying CAT. You may take a gift from several people in the same calendar year, and the first €3,000 from each disponer (the person making the gift) is exempt from CAT.

How can I reduce taxes on inheritance and gifts?
A Section 72 policy is a type of life-insurance policy that parents (usually) can buy to pay their children's inheritance tax bill. The policy works much the same as a regular life-insurance policy,

but is set up under trust for the beneficiaries. It is designed to pay the children sufficient money on death to meet any inheritance taxes that arise. This policy is to provide a lump sum at death, which will be used to pay the tax bill. This lump sum is also not counted as part of the estate and is exempt from CAT.

Unlike the Section 72, which is paid on death, assets must be gifted before death of the policy owner on a Section 73. This enables an annual amount to be invested, which will appreciate.

Capital Gains Tax

What is Capital Gains Tax?
Capital Gains Tax (CGT) is charged on the profits from the 'disposal' (usually sale) of certain assets, such as property, shares or other investments. A flat tax rate of 33% is charged for disposals. For example, if you profit from selling an investment property (not your primary residence or home), you pay CGT.

You are considered as having disposed of an asset if you sell it, gift it, exchange it or get compensation or insurance for it.

When do I pay CGT?
The dates to pay and file CGT are based on the date you sold, gifted or transferred an asset. For disposals made between:
- 1 January and 30 November (the initial period), you must pay CGT by 15 December of the same year.
- 1 December and 31 December (the later period), you must pay CGT by 31 January of the following year.

How do I reduce CGT?

- Any money you spend that adds value to the asset (known as 'enhancement expenditure') can be deducted from the sales price of the investment.
- Costs, such as fees paid to a solicitor or auctioneer when you acquired and disposed of the asset, can be deducted from the sales price of the investment.
- When you have calculated your chargeable gain on the asset, you can reduce your liability by deducting a tax credit called the 'annual personal exemption', which amounts to €1,270.
- If you make a loss when you dispose of an asset, this is known as an 'allowable loss'. You can deduct an allowable loss from any CGT owed in the same tax year. This can include losses on the disposal of foreign property.
- You may carry forward the losses. This means you can use them against a capital gain you make in later years. You can also use the balance against gains made by your spouse or civil partner.
- Other exemptions and reliefs, such as retirement relief, can also reduce the amount of CGT you are liable to pay. Seek financial advice if you are unsure about your CGT obligations.

Other taxes

What is exit tax?

Exit tax is applied to the growth in value of some life-assurance policies and investment funds when the investor 'exits' the fund. It amounts to 41% of the growth.

The life-assurance companies – Zurich Life or Aviva Life – are ultimately responsible for calculating and paying the exit tax on life-assurance policies rather than the investor, though you may be required to calculate and pay the exit tax yourself on some investment funds.

Even if you haven't physically sold or disposed of your investment, you could still be subject to tax on the growth in value of your investment, generally every eight years. This is called 'imputed disposal'. Revenue created this tax legislation during the recession in 2008 as a way for them to get tax from investments that weren't being cashed in. We have to hand it to Revenue – they are creative in taxing people.

It is important to consult with a good financial planner when investing – as you can see, tax regulations can impact the overall return on your investment.

What is Deposit Interest Retention Tax?

Deposit Interest Retention Tax (DIRT) is applied to interest earned from savings in banks, building societies or credit unions. These institutions deduct DIRT at source, meaning the interest you receive already has the tax deducted. The current DIRT rate for 2024 is 33%.

People aged over sixty-five, as well as those who are permanently incapacitated, may not have to pay DIRT. They must fill in the relevant forms, which allow the bank to pay the interest to them without deducting DIRT.

Those not resident in Ireland are also not liable to pay DIRT but, again, they need to inform their bank or financial institution.

How can I get organised for tax?

Both self-employed and PAYE workers need to keep on top of a lot of income and expenses and various deductions to reduce their tax bills.

A lot of PAYE workers also have a side hustle these days. I have clients who are dance teachers or music teachers on the side. Others are paid to coach kids' football at weekends and others sell online. That's all earned income and must be declared for tax purposes.

Of course, the expenses incurred by these businesses will help reduce that tax bill. But to ensure you get all the reductions and reliefs you're entitled to, you need to be organised and track all your incomings and outgoings.

Many apps are available to help you do this but, often, my clients don't like using them. Some apps are too complicated and some people have privacy concerns about apps. You feed these apps with a lot of information, especially if you have any medical complaints and are submitting medical expenses.

Do what I do instead. Set up a Gmail address to send and store all your expenses. For example, if your name is Sean Murphy, set up an address called seanmurphyreceipts2024@gmail.com.

Everyone carries a smartphone these days, making it effortless to take a quick photograph or shot of a receipt wherever you are. Then, you just send the receipt to your Gmail account. Make it easier by adding the details in the subject line: 'Sean doctor fee €60'. At the end of the year, just log in to your Gmail account, and you'll see an accurate list of all your expenses.

You must keep these receipts for Revenue for at least seven years, so you'll also have the assurance they're safe in the cloud.

Examples of expense receipts to keep:

- **Medical and dental expenses**: You can claim tax relief on certain medical and dental expenses not covered by the state or private health insurance.
- **Tuition fees**: You may also claim relief on tuition fees paid for approved courses.
- **Home renovations**: Tax relief may be available for homeowners who carry out renovation and improvement works on their main home through the Home Renovation Incentive Scheme.
- **Pension contributions**: Contributions to personal or occupational pension schemes can reduce your overall tax liability.
- **Expenses for rental income**: If you own rental property, certain expenses can be deducted before calculating your taxable income, including maintenance and repair expenses, insurance, property management fees, and mortgage interest under certain conditions.
- **Expenses for self-employed**: Certain expenses can be deducted from your tax liability, including phone bills, protective clothing, website costs, fuel, parking and other motor expenses, office expenses, accountancy fees and rent.

Your 7-point action plan for tax

- Organise your financial information throughout the year. Gather invoices, investment income statements, receipts for deductible expenses, health costs, etc. as you go. Organisation is vital for a smooth and accurate tax-filing process. See the Gmail tip above to help organise your tax affairs.

- Check your Tax Credit Certificate. Ensure you get all the tax credits you're entitled to.
- Understand your tax bands and know the different tax bands and credits available.
- Make sure to declare income from all sources. This includes income from a job, self-employment, rental income, investment returns, etc. If you leave out income, it can lead to expensive fines from Revenue and missed opportunities for deductions.
- Stay on top of the allowances and reliefs you are entitled to. Certain medical expenses, dental work, tuition fees, pension contributions and rental expenses are all deductible.
- Remember to meet your tax deadlines. The late filing of a tax return can result in penalties or fines. The tax return deadline for self-assessed individuals is 31 October.
- Seek professional advice if you find filing tax overwhelming. A tax consultant, accountant or financial planner can advise for your circumstances.

SECTION 5
FINANCIAL PROTECTION

I'm really passionate about financial protection planning, and I try to instil the same fervour in all my team. I've even worked on creating software so the finance industry can do a better job of protecting our clients. I cannot overemphasise enough the importance of getting good financial protection for life's unexpected events.

This passion for protecting people's lives comes from several places and experiences during my own lifetime.

I've lost people close to me, several of them were young. Some of these deaths were expected after long illnesses but others were tragically unexpected. What family or person hasn't been touched by serious conditions, such as strokes, cancer or heart attacks? I've witnessed the aftermath of families struggling.

Dealing with grief is hard, and you don't need the added turmoil of mounting debts and financial troubles.

I've also met people unable to return to their professions, where they trained for years. They are architects, nurses and engineers who can never work again in their field because of illness or injury. Some wrongly believed their job would pay them indefinitely if they got sick or were injured. I've seen businesses collapse after losing a key person. Sometimes, the entire company rests on one or two people, and their loss is disastrous.

All that was required to prevent these scenarios was a simple conversation which starts with the question: 'What happens if something happens to me?'

I'm also aware that the general public has a poor awareness of state benefits. Did you know that if you are a cohabiting couple, you will not get the widow's or widower's pension should your partner pass away?

In 1995, only 8% of children were born outside of a formal marriage. It's now closer to 40%. If you needed another reason to bring forward the wedding, state benefits might be it – especially when you've children.

So many people have a lot to protect, yet they have no backup when things go badly. I get frustrated with the banking sector's failure to focus on people's protection needs. They establish a case for a mortgage, a pension or investment instead of stepping back and looking at a client's overall circumstances. I meet people who think they have good protection policies in place, but when I look at them, they're not suitable at all.

I've seen life, in all its glory, come with its fair share of uncertainties, tragedies and unexpected events. Having a protection plan in place is essential for financial well-being and security. It's the cavalry that races over the hill to rescue you or your family when an unforeseen calamity arises. Everyone needs a financial protection plan.

What is a financial protection plan?

A financial protection plan contains measures to reduce the impact of an unexpected calamity on finances. Most people already have some broader insurance measures. If you own your own home, you'll have home insurance. Families often have private health insurance to cover medical expenses and costs for hospital stays, surgeries, consultants and routine doctor visits.

If you buy your home with a bank loan, you must have mortgage protection. This form of insurance is required by law in Ireland and pays off your mortgage if you die during the policy term.

However, we often forget to insure the two most important things:

- The person who pays for these insurances – that's you.
- Your income that pays for everything.

Any good financial protection plan should focus on insuring you and your income.

Why do we need protection?

Most, if not all of us, have plenty to protect – which is a positive thing. Protecting ourselves is the frontline in the financial-planning process. The two most significant stressors in life are health and money. When you can avoid one of these for a small cost, why wouldn't you?

Imagine this: you've been working hard, building a life for yourself and your family. You have a lovely home and your children are set to go to university, but, suddenly, life takes an unforeseen turn. The mere thought of this can be distressing, but maybe you are diagnosed with a serious illness. Maybe you're hurt in a car accident. For whatever reason, you're no longer able to work. What happens? The bills pile up and, suddenly, paying for the children's education seems like a mountain to climb. You can no longer meet the mortgage repayments or the finance for the car.

But misfortunes don't have to turn into financial disasters as well. It's bad enough having to deal with illness, injury or a death in the family. The right insurance plan can offer financial assistance should bad things happen.

Simply put, a good financial protection plan can secure financial stability, absorb economic shocks from unexpected life events and offer peace of mind. It's an essential part of your financial well-being.

Some good reasons for a protection plan

- A protection plan can safeguard your family's future should you die. If you are the primary earner and pass away unexpectedly, you can leave dependants financially vulnerable. A life-insurance policy ensures they receive a lump sum or regular payments to help with living expenses.

- Financial protection products can also help pay off outstanding debts upon your death. They ensure these obligations don't fall on other family members.
- Accidents or illnesses can strike at any time and prevent us from working for a prolonged period. Income-protection insurance provides a regular income during this time.
- Specified serious-illness cover can also provide a financial buffer during a health crisis.
- Business partners should always have a protection plan in case one of them dies or becomes incapacitated.

Do you have phone or gadget insurance?

A Central Bank survey in 2018 found that 440,000 people in Ireland had gadget insurance. I wonder how those 440,000 people would pay for that insurance if they were too sick or injured to work.

The finance industry has communicated the importance and affordability of good protection planning poorly. We have lost the insurance war to other forms of insurance that are better marketed to you.

Many people have health insurance even though it's expensive. However, they haven't even asked for a quotation on income protection to rescue them if they can't work.

Is your computer insured? Are your pets insured? Do you have breakdown insurance on your television or washing machine? Many people pay hefty sums for these protections, yet they haven't insured the most important item in their lives – themselves. Are you really going to prioritise insurance for an iPhone for €20 a month? Are you going to insure your pet over your own income or health?

I am not telling you that something catastrophic will happen – it is more likely that it won't. However, the cost to you will be disastrous if something does happen. The cost of protection is almost insignificant if it neutralises this financial threat to you.

In my financial-planning business, we address protection with clients early on. You may come to us with another agenda, but I see this as something you need to consider when you start earning. I regard it as part of our duty of care to address protection first. It may be treated as an afterthought for customers in other financial institutions. Not with us.

Quiz

Insurance cover

How much does €1 million life cover cost for a non-smoking, thirty-seven-year-old man for the next twenty-five years?

You probably won't know, nor should you, but I can guarantee that most of you will drastically overestimate the cost.

This life-insurance policy will pay a lump sum of €1 million to this man's partner and dependants if he dies. (Let's make it clear: it's unlikely you'll need €1 million in cover – I've arbitrarily picked this sum because it's a vast round number.) As of the end of 2023, this cover costs around €84 per month.

What kinds of financial protection are there?

The three key protection pillars are life insurance, income protection and critical illness insurance. Let's briefly focus on each one.

1. Life insurance

Life insurance provides a lump-sum payment or regular income to your dependants or estate upon your death. This replaces your lost income to the household and covers general living expenses and education costs.

2. Income protection

This policy offers a regular income if you cannot work for a prolonged period of time because of injury or illness. It is a financial bridge until you can return to work or retire. This is often known as salary protection. It's an essential safety net, especially for those who are self-employed or whose jobs don't provide sick pay.

3. Specified serious-illness cover

Specified serious-illness cover (also known as critical-illness cover) provides a tax-free, lump-sum payment if you're diagnosed with a serious illness covered by the policy. It can help you cover medical and living expenses while you are recovering.

How does protection planning change with age?

I have different protection conversations with my clients depending on their age and whether or not they're parents. With business owners, there's a separate conversation to be had too.

Parents with young children need to focus on life insurance to provide for the family after death. This is not a priority for anyone without children.

Most clients in their twenties, thirties and forties are far more likely to get sick or injured in their working lives than they are to die. As a result, income protection is most important when your earning power is at its height.

The need for protection diminishes for people in their fifties and sixties as they get closer to retirement and any children become older. Pensions take priority, and protection planning in these years shifts to legacy or estate planning.

Why do so many people fail to consider a protection plan?

I see people who shrug when I broach the subject of getting a financial protection plan in place. And these can be parents of young children who are self-employed and more desperately in need of a protection plan than anyone else.

- Most of us (myself included) have a tendency towards self-delusion, avoidance or misplaced optimism. We often have an 'it won't happen to me' attitude. Somehow, we believe we're immune to becoming ill, getting injured or dying prematurely. We often think we're bulletproof, especially up to our forties.
- Lack of awareness about financial protection plans is definitely an issue. Many people don't even know that these products are available or how they provide security in times of crisis.
- Many people prioritise their current needs and don't look towards the future. This is understandable when you're up

to your eyes in work and paying bills. Many find keeping up with daily life so difficult that they neglect long-term financial planning.

- Some people perceive insurance as expensive and don't even investigate their options. They assume, wrongly in most cases, that they can't afford the premiums.

- Some people have a naïve belief that social welfare and benefits will adequately cover them in times of need, even though they only provide basic cover. Unfortunately, illness and injury can dramatically increase your cost of living, and what you get from the state will not meet those costs.

- I also face a lot of plain old procrastination regarding protection planning. I have clients who recognise the need for a financial protection plan but keep delaying it, prioritising other expenses. 'I'll do it next year, Paul …'

Some reasons you should reconsider protection

I don't like scaremongering, but consider the following data.

- We've researched thousands of our new clients from askpaul.ie since 2020. Our research reveals that 75% of them would not survive financially for six months without an income. They admit their savings would be decimated by then. How would you score here?

- The average life-assurance policy payout in Ireland is only €50,000–€66,000, which won't go far for the family you leave behind. Life assurance itself is not the issue, the problem is many people hold policies with insufficient cover in place. Please seek advice.

- The average breast cancer diagnosis is at age forty-two.
- Men, on average, die five years earlier than women.
- If you're eligible, the state illness benefit is only €232 a week (or €928 a month). This will not fund most people's mortgages if they cannot work.
- The financial cost of losing a stay-at-home parent is often grossly underestimated. The cost to employ someone to perform the same duties as a stay-at-home parent is estimated to be over €47,000, according to a 2020 iReach survey.

What are the odds of serious illness or death?

For simplicity, let's look at the probabilities of serious illness for Joe and Jane Bloggs in the next twenty-seven years until they retire, using Aviva's risk check calculator.

Aged forty-one, both are non-smokers and plan to work until the age of sixty-eight, which will soon be the new retirement age.

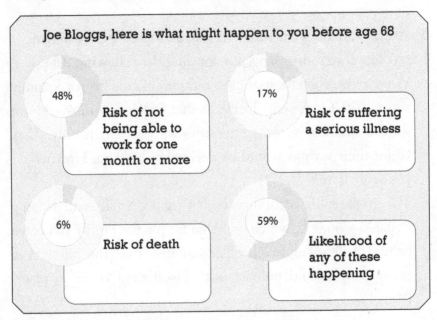

Joe Bloggs, here is what might happen to you before age 68

48% Risk of not being able to work for one month or more

17% Risk of suffering a serious illness

6% Risk of death

59% Likelihood of any of these happening

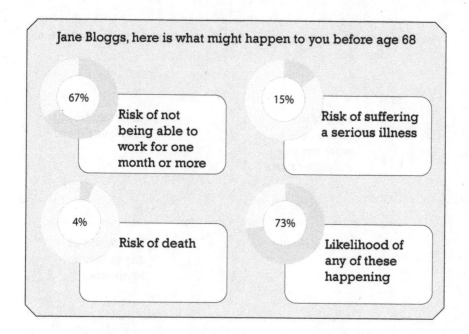

Jane Bloggs, here is what might happen to you before age 68

67% — Risk of not being able to work for one month or more

15% — Risk of suffering a serious illness

4% — Risk of death

73% — Likelihood of any of these happening

What do these comparisons tell us?

Firstly, when it comes to death and illness, gender impacts in different ways:

- Jane has less of a chance of dying in those twenty-seven years.
- Joe has a higher probability of a severe illness in those twenty-seven years.
- Jane has a significantly higher chance of being out of work for one month or more during those years.

Ideally, we would devise a plan to protect Joe and Jane Bloggs against these scenarios within a budget. What happens if Joe and Jane Bloggs fall in love and come to see me as a couple? The probabilities of these scenarios combine and change.

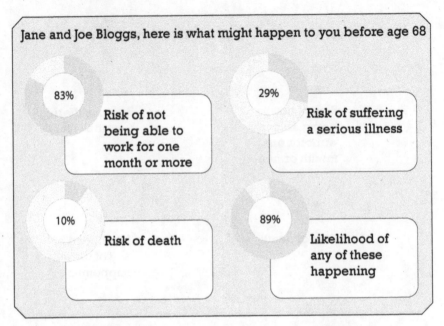

Jane and Joe Bloggs, here is what might happen to you before age 68

83% — Risk of not being able to work for one month or more

29% — Risk of suffering a serious illness

10% — Risk of death

89% — Likelihood of any of these happening

Hopefully, these graphs and statistics have triggered a greater awareness of the need for financial protection planning.

How hard is it to maintain a protection plan?

Protection planning is not the most pleasant part of a financial plan – it's the 'worry' part. Even though it's the frontline of financial planning, it's simple when you have put a plan in place.

The beauty of a protection plan is that if you set it up right at the outset, it requires minimal effort after that. It's not like a pension or investments that need constant reviewing. It doesn't require consideration like a mortgage, where you have to decide what to do after you come off that fixed rate next year …

Do you need to review your protection plan periodically? Absolutely, but not every year. Call the askpaul team and ask for a plan to be put in place.

Who offers protection policies in Ireland?

The following five leading life-assurance companies offer protection products in Ireland:

- Aviva Life & Pensions
- Irish Life
- New Ireland
- Royal London
- Zurich Life

Between these five companies, you have many products and significant price variations to choose from, which makes it challenging to choose the right products for your circumstances. Any good financial planner working within a brokerage should have access to the products from all five life assurance companies. They'll also have a good working knowledge of all the products on offer.

What are the common triggers for seeking protection?

From my experience with clients, the following are the main reasons people consider protection:

- We're just after getting our mortgage signed off. The bank is making us take out mortgage protection. Do we have to take it? Do we have to take their policy? We wanted to check with you.
- Oh my god, I have just had a child. I am responsible for someone else. What do I do to secure their future?
- I've been worrying about this. I need to protect my income, but other financial priorities pushed it down the line. I'm ready to start now.

- I'm starting a business or building a business. How do I protect it?
- We're doing a fundraiser for a guy we used to work with. What can I do so I never end up in the same position?
- I want to look after my kids when I'm gone. Tell me about estate planning.

CLIENT CASE

LEO & CATHERINE, AGED 41 & 38

Leo and Catherine had their first child in 2015 and came to me to sort out some life cover. As renters, they felt they needed insurance in case anything happened to either of them. They paid €80 in total for life cover of €375,000 each if either died.

In 2017, they bought a house and bought the mandatory mortgage protection. They now had life insurance to protect each other as breadwinners and a mortgage policy to clear the mortgage in the event of either's death.

A while later, the couple came to me again. Leo had landed a new job in a multinational with good benefits, including life cover for employees. They thought they might drop the €80 policy as they wanted to cut down on a few expenses to pay for hefty bills like crèche fees.

I reminded Leo that he would probably switch jobs every four to five years. (The average person will now have seven different employments in their lifespan.) He may or may not get life cover in his next job.

He was now forty-one. If they lapsed the €80 a month policy, they would be in their mid-forties and getting new life cover would be more expensive. In the meantime, they would be refused life cover if an ailment or injury happened to either.

They both decided that they couldn't afford to be without the cover. It amounted to €40 each a month, and the benefits and peace of mind outweighed any benefits of this cost-cutting exercise.

CLIENT CASE
PETER & SARAH, AGED 39

Peter and Sarah have two children under the age of five. They have a comprehensive protection plan covering them for most eventualities, including mandatory mortgage protection, which costs them €129 a month each. I think it's a lot of peace of mind for not a huge amount of money. Their plan consists of:

- **Life assurance**: Cost €67 per month – they are not married, so they will not get the widow's or widower's pensions if either were to die – they are insured for €360,000 each
- **Income protection policy for Peter**: Cost €55 per month after tax relief
- **Income protection policy for Sarah**: Cost €41 per month after tax relief

- **Mortgage protection policy**: Cost €44 per month for their €395,000 home
- **Specified serious-illness cover for Peter**: Cost €26 per month – pays out a lump sum of €70,000 should he get severely ill
- **Specified serious-illness cover for Sarah**: Cost €25 per month – pays out a lump sum of €60,000 should she get severely ill

Their total monthly cost, including mortgage protection, is €258 for the couple. Their combined after-tax income is €8,700 per month, so protection costs for the couple and their earnings amount to 3% of their monthly budget.

What are living benefits versus death benefits?

The odds of either Joe or Jane Bloggs dying before retirement is only 10%. However, it's still a bit too high for their liking.

Death is a catastrophic event. You should use a life-cover policy to aggressively protect against the potential fallout from the loss of your spouse.

However, industry claims and actuary research prove it's far more probable that the Bloggs (and people in their age demographic of over forty to retirement age) are far more likely to get severely sick or injured. We've all seen colleagues out sick for long periods or friends or relatives struck down by unexpected injuries or illness.

If I have to choose, I will use a limited budget to pay for living benefits rather than death benefits. If a client has a budget of €100 a month, I would advise living benefits over death benefits.

What are living benefits?

Living benefits are protection policies that protect against severe illness and injury and come under two types of protection policies:

- income-protection cover
- specified serious-illness cover

What is income-protection cover?

I'll always list income protection first. Why? Because your income is your most valuable asset and protecting it is vital.

Income protection insurance says it like it is – it protects your income or salary. It provides you with a reliable source of income (taxable like any income) in the unfortunate event that you cannot work because of an accident or illness. With this coverage, you have peace of mind knowing you can meet your mortgage, household bills and living expenses even in the worst times.

Why is income my most valuable asset?

We often consider physical assets – such as houses, cars or savings – as our greatest assets. In reality, your ability to earn an income is your most substantial asset.

Let's take Simon. He's thirty-nine, has children and a mortgage, and works in the private sector. His gross salary is €60,000 a year and he expects this to grow in the coming years through annual raises, promotions, etc.

He hopes to retire at sixty-six, so he has twenty-seven years of his working life left. Let's say for simplicity's sake that Simon never gets a pay increase for the next twenty-seven years, so his salary remains at €60,000.

His salary is worth: €60,000 x 27 years = €1.62 million

Simon may have a house and car and a good investment fund, but nothing comes close to his income in terms of value. His income is his most valuable financial asset by far.

You and your earning power fuel your life. Yet, most clients I meet do not have income protection.

They all have home insurance if they are homeowners. But your house is not as important as your income. You don't own your home until you clear the mortgage. Even then, it's not a liquid asset. A home is rarely realised as a financial asset in your lifetime as you always need a place to live.

When I first meet clients, they may also have some life cover. They will sometimes have a pension from work, and they may have phone or gadget insurance. However, they rarely think about the importance of protecting their income. An injury or a health crisis could render any of us unable to work and threaten our future financial well-being.

The truth is your income is your wealth and pays for everything in your life. If you had a machine that manufactured €3,500 a month for you, I have no doubt you would insure it. You are that incredible machine, and you should guarantee your ability to keep producing that money.

It baffles me when people ignore income protection – I'm not exaggerating when I say it keeps me awake at night.

Why do renters need income protection even more?

Over 1 million people in Ireland live in rented accommodation. These renters are no longer the traditional mix of students and singles in their twenties and thirties. Today, we have many older people and married couples with children in rental accommodation.

People in long-term rental accommodation are more exposed than homeowners if they cannot pay the rent. This is because homeowners have mortgage-arrear processes and legal protections that can prolong the eviction process. Also, there is greater flexibility with payment holidays or interest-only payments.

Any person in rental accommodation needs to focus on an income-protection policy as a priority.

What you need to know when setting up a protection plan

When designing a protection plan for clients, I need to know their current financial situation. Most clients can survive three to six months without an income. During this time, they use savings and may get full- or half-pay from their employer. It's when it goes beyond this they are in trouble.

These details are important. For example, if you get help from your employer for three months, you can defer income protection and get cheaper cover. You can set a deferred period from between four to fifty-two weeks on some income-protection policies. The longer the delay, the cheaper your cover will be.

These are some questions you need to answer:

- Do you have any employment benefits in your job? Do these benefits include income protection? If you're unsure, check with your employer.

- Do you know how long your employer will pay if you are off work because of illness?
- How much will they pay?
- Are you eligible for full state benefits, such as illness benefit?
- What have you saved for a rainy day? How long will this last you without pay?
- Do you really want to decimate your savings if you have them?
- What is your annual *net* salary?
- How much do you need to survive?
- How much protection can you afford? (It's always better to protect some of your income than none.)

Why do I advocate income protection so strongly?

It's like car insurance. When you start out driving, you're young and broke, and all you can afford is third party, fire and theft. As you get older, you have more cash. The car improves, and you move to fully comprehensive car insurance.

Income protection for me is the fully comp of financial-planning products. It's the real belt-and-braces approach to financial planning. It insures your greatest asset – your income – in case the day comes that you cannot do your job. You will have an income stream that is guaranteed until you recover or retire.

You also receive tax relief when paying for income protection. The government actually gives you financial help to buy income-protection insurance. If you pay the higher tax rate, the Revenue Commissioners effectively pay 40% of your premium. This means if my income protection premium is €100, I only have to pay €60. The government isn't doing this out of the goodness of its heart.

A critically ill person with no income can be a heavy burden on the state.

I always advocate for income protection because I have seen these policies work at the worst of times. No one ever wants to claim income protection, but they do.

I have clients who were forced out of work through no fault of their own. Thankfully, however, their lives have not been completely devastated as they had backup. They had the cavalry riding over that hill. They have income protection. The last thing anyone wants in a health crisis is a financial crisis.

Is income protection for everyone?

No, it isn't for everyone. If you work in the home, income protection cannot properly quantify your monetary value. It's the same if you only work part-time. Income protection is linked to formal salaried income.

Income protection can also be more expensive for some workers. Jobs with a greater risk of injury have higher costs for income-protection insurance. Physical work – like construction and jobs involving heavy machinery, working at heights or in hazardous environments – makes policies more expensive.

In some cases, you may not be able to get insurance – the life-assurance company may consider your occupation or hobbies too risky. However, specified serious-illness cover can provide protections for those who can't get access to income protection.

What is specified serious-illness cover?

Specified serious-illness cover (or critical-illness cover) offers protection against an unexpected health scare. This policy provides a tax-free, lump-sum payment that is paid out if you're diagnosed with a serious illness covered by the policy. These illnesses can include cancer, heart attack, stroke, etc. It can help cover extra medical and living expenses while out of work, getting treatment and recovering.

Serious-illness cover will provide help with the following.

- Your immediate loss of income and paying household bills.
- Your loss of productivity and inability to work in the home or to work part time. It can provide money for help in the home.
- The costs of your health treatment, seeing consultants and paying for hospital parking fees. (If you've had extensive dealings with a hospital, you know how the parking fees mount up.)
- Giving you time to recover after treatment.
- Therapy and rehabilitation bills.
- Enabling a holiday for you and your loved ones after a challenging period.

What's the difference between income protection and serious-illness cover?

Income-protection cover

This is the long-term hedge. It's a strategy to secure your financial stability over an extended period. If you're too sick or injured to return to work, it can pay you a salary until retirement age, when your pension kicks in. By paying for income protection, you're hedging against the risk of a prolonged income loss in the future.

Serious-illness cover

This is the short-term hedge. This provides a lump-sum payment if you're diagnosed with a specific illness listed within your policy. The aim is to cover immediate financial needs after a critical-illness diagnosis. The payout can help cover your loss of income and pay the bills and other necessary expenses. It's 'short term' because it offers a one-off payout to manage immediate costs. A tax-free lump sum of €70,000 may provide an excellent financial buffer for a year or two, but it's not the solution for long-term illness or injury.

What are the disadvantages of specified serious-illness cover?

- It's a one-off lump-sum payment, not designed for long-term support.
- Specified serious-illness policies can be expensive if you want large amounts of cover. Obtaining €250,000 worth of illness cover is not affordable for most. This is where your money should be funnelled into income protection. I usually advise one or two years' *net* salary as a guideline for serious-illness cover.
- This product can be overly complicated. The definitions of illness are difficult to comprehend if you're not a medical professional. Yet, I see these insurances being sold online.
- We see a wild variation in the quality of policies in the marketplace. Policies can change several times in a year. This is where financial advice adds a lot of value. Planners can stay on top of these changes.
- Specified serious-illness cover comes with the qualifying word 'specified'. This means the cover is limited. You won't

receive a payout if you fall seriously ill with a condition that is not on the policy's list. Not all cancers are covered, for example.

- Also, most serious-illness policies will not cover pre-existing conditions. If you already have a medical condition when you take out the policy, complications arising from that condition will most likely not be covered.

- Banks sometimes sell this product wrapped in a mortgage-protection policy. I don't like this. If there is a claim, the money goes to the bank first, not you. Always get serious-illness cover on a stand-alone basis.

- Specified serious-illness cover also gets expensive as you get older. The premiums can rise significantly with age, lifestyle choices and your current health.

- Some policies have a waiting period before you can make a claim, so if you're diagnosed within that period, no benefits will be paid out. Many policies have a 'survival period', meaning you must survive for a certain period (usually fourteen days) after diagnosis before a claim can be paid out.

- Specified serious-illness premiums are not tax deductible, unlike income protection.

What are the serious-illness claims for men and women?

- Around 72% of claims for women are cancer related.
- Around 50% of claims for men are stroke/heart attack related.

Gender differences are really significant. This should shape your priorities when trying to find the right serious-illness cover.

What are death benefits?

We've already discussed 'living benefits' that are paid out if you have the misfortune to become seriously ill, injured or permanently disabled. These come in the form of income-protection and specified serious-illness policies. Death benefits arise when the worst happens. It is the nuclear button of insurance and the one that no one wants to use.

Thankfully, it's also the most unlikely thing to happen during your working life, but it is so catastrophic to loved ones who are left behind that it should be an essential part of every earner's protection plan.

Death benefits are a payout to your beneficiaries upon your death. The most common type of insurance that provides death benefits is life insurance. Some people may have life cover through their employer, known as death-in-service benefit. This is often linked to their pension scheme. However, death-in-service benefits are usually limited and capped in value.

What are the problems with DIY life insurance?

Where do I begin here? I see a lot of DIY financial planning when it comes to life insurance. Clients buy policies online or are sold policies by someone with no experience in financial advice. As a result, I see clients who:

- are underinsured
- pay too much and are overinsured
- didn't disclose information correctly, so their families were denied their claims

- let valuable policies lapse at the wrong time
- overpay for poor policies
- hold on to policies with reviewable premiums that only go one way ... up.
- forget they have policies.

Of course, I also have clients who prefer to disregard their responsibilities and have no life insurance at all.

Twelve questions all life-insurance holders should answer

1. Do you understand the life-insurance policy you have?
2. Do you know who it is with?
3. Do you know where the policy documents are?
4. Do you know what cover you have?
5. Is illness cover wrapped into your policy?
6. Do you know if it's linked to your mortgage protection?
7. Does the premium change?
8. Is it good value?
9. Do your loved ones know about it?
10. Do they know how to claim if you pass away?
11. Who manages this claim if you have young children and no surviving parents?
12. Have you made a will?

If, like many people, you don't know the answers to these questions, you need an urgent review of your protection plan. You need to check that the monthly direct debit you pay will provide for your family should they ever need to make a claim.

What are the positives of having life insurance?

- It is inexpensive – providing financial peace of mind for minimal cost.
- There are huge variations to suit a lot of circumstances. Some cover income only; others are products with tax rebates; others let you extend cover.
- You can insure each other as a couple.
- Processing a valid claim is not difficult. More than 95% of claims made on life insurance are successful.
- The premiums are fixed but increase if you need additional cover because of life changes, such as having more children, bigger salaries, etc.
- Life cover is the bedrock of a good financial plan to protect your loved ones.

How much life cover do I need?

You may consider this a politician's reply – we consider many factors when deciding how much life cover you need.

It really depends on you and your unique situation. Important criteria include the following.

- Your monthly take-home pay.
- The number of children you have and how old they are. I usually aim to provide coverage until the youngest child is twenty-five. This gives enough cover to meet modern education needs and the fact adult children often can't afford to live away from home.
- Does your employer contribute to a death-in-service benefit?
- Does your mortgage protection have any policy benefit left over for your dependants after paying off the mortgage?

- Your current savings.
- Your budget for insurance.
- What's the cost of replacing each parent in the event of death? Different roles have different financial impacts on a family.
- Health-screening advancements can cause more complications when seeking life cover. More genetic conditions or potential health risks are being identified. This affects an individual's eligibility for certain life-insurance policies and the cost of premiums.

Many pluck a figure out of the sky for life-insurance cover. They request cover for a hefty six- or seven-figure sum for a random twenty-year term.

It's vital to take a more analytical approach to choosing a policy. A good financial planner will guide you through this process.

Unfortunately, people often treat life policies differently from other insurance policies like their home, health or car insurance. These insurance policies are reviewed and repriced annually, while life policies are commonly bought once and then forgotten.

There's a tendency to shove it in a drawer or stick it in that 'folder' that gathers dust. People will work hard to save €100 on car insurance but won't take the time to review a policy that could be worth hundreds of thousands or could leave you vastly underinsured.

Don't let this be you – make sure your life-insurance policy suits you and your loved ones. I recommend people review their protection policies, both living expenses and death benefits, every three years.

What about life insurance and complicated modern families?

Sorting out life insurance becomes more complex when you consider modern family dynamics. These complications can include:

- the breakdown of relationships
- unmarried couples and inheritance rights
- multiple families and determining beneficiaries after a death
- complexities of inheritance rights
- family trusts
- planning the adult lives for children with special needs.

Addressing these issues isn't usually difficult when the policyholder is alive, but it becomes a significant problem if we try to sort it out after they have died.

I've seen the fallout of these situations with life-insurance policies and wish the policyholder had taken the time to address the complexities of their situation. Considering these potential complications is essential if you want your life insurance to benefit your loved ones.

Life cover in my business

Making a life claim on behalf of the bereaved families of my clients is a bittersweet experience. It is one of the most satisfying and, at the same time, most difficult parts of my job.

Often, families don't even know about the life cover they are due. It's one final, unexpected gift from their departed loved one. But they really appreciate our role in this matter, as we help remove one obstacle in their difficult journey ahead.

Private health insurance

What is private health insurance?

Private health insurance is a policy that covers some or all of your medical costs if you get sick or injured. You pay a monthly premium, and they cover your medical expenses according to the terms of your policy.

In Ireland, we have a mix of public and private healthcare. Many worry about their access to public healthcare, given the long waiting lists and overcrowded hospitals. We fear we won't get the care required when we need it. This is where private health insurance can step in, providing access to private hospitals and specialists.

Not all health-insurance plans are created equally. Premiums, excess amounts and waiting periods can vary, so it's important to decide what matters most to you in a health-insurance plan.

Why is private health insurance so popular in Ireland?

From the outset, I want to say I'm an advocate of private health insurance and always have been. None of us are strangers to the horror stories of the three-year waiting lists for vital procedures or treatments.

However, I often wish we as a society had the same love for retirement planning or protecting a business or loved ones as we do for health insurance.

As of the end of 2022, circa 2.44 million or nearly half of the population in Ireland (47%) had private health insurance. This compares with around 10% of the population in the UK.

So why have we embraced health insurance and yet so few of us protect our income if we get sick or injured?

Private health insurance takes priority here for cultural, historical and practical reasons.

The VHI, which has the largest health insurance market share, is a semi-state institution heavily ingrained into our society's fabric.

Established in 1957, many of our grandparents and parents had policies. As children, our parents insured us on VHI, so we grew up with health insurance. Employment benefits have traditionally been linked to health insurance too.

However, concerns about access to and quality of care in the public healthcare system prompt most of us to shell out for health insurance today.

The health budget increases each year, yet overcrowded public hospitals and lengthy waiting lists continue. And the perception is private insurance allows you to bypass public waiting lists and receive quicker treatment.

As a result, even though private health insurance is not a cheap product, many will drop other direct debits before health insurance.

Who are the private health insurers?

We have three key players, all aggressive competitors, offering many solutions for your medical care.

- VHI
- Irish Life
- Laya Healthcare

Why research your health-insurance policy every year?

Like all providers of financial services, health-insurance companies rely on customers' inertia and complacency to boost their profits. They love the 'auto-renewal' method of selling annual policies. It saves them time and hassle, but it means you are paying more than you need to for cover.

Many companies have older 'legacy' plans that people keep renewing year after year. The companies hike the prices on those old policies bought by their most loyal members and introduce similar but more competitively priced new policies to attract new customers.

Health-insurance policies are not cheap; we should continually review them to keep costs down. Some of you will have health insurance as part of your benefits at work. However, this benefit may disappear as more companies cut costs and health-insurance costs keep rising. Many who never considered health-insurance costs in the past may soon have to factor in the hefty cost of insurance into their net pay.

This is even more reason to compare prices and watch for new, more competitively priced policies. You cannot lock in health-insurance premiums like you can with life cover or income protection. You are at the mercy of the market, so you must play the game.

How do you compare health-insurance policies?

The askpaul team doesn't advise in this specialised area of insurance. I explored health insurance in an episode of my financial podcast, *Two Pauls in a Pod*, in 2023. I talked with industry colleague Dermot Goode of Total Health Cover, which specialises in health insurance. He's a real authority in the field, and you can hear it on Spotify or wherever you get your podcasts.

Compare the vast market of health-insurance policies yourself on the government-funded Health Insurance Authority website (www.hia.ie), which is a treasure trove of free information for the consumer. The HIA allows you to compare plans by:

- age
- demographics

It also enables you to compare your existing plan against the market and to compare multiple plans simultaneously.

The two basic types of cover in most private health-insurance policies are:

- **Hospital cover**: This pays for both outpatient services and when admitted to hospital. The policy can cover all or some treatments, surgery, scans, tests, and overnight stays.
- **Everyday medical expenses**: This covers GP and consultant visits, opticians, some dental costs and therapies, including physio, chiropody, reflexology, etc.

Does the cost of health insurance rise with age?

One of the great benefits of health insurance in Ireland is that providers can't raise the cost of premiums because you're older. Nor can they penalise you for switching.

Many older people fear switching in case their premium rises or they lose benefits as they age. However, Irish health insurers are not allowed to discriminate by age. The HIA calls it 'risk equalisation', and they financially compensate the three providers for the additional costs of insuring older and less healthy members.

However, there *are* penalties for those aged thirty-five or above who buy health insurance for *the first time*. The older you are when you first buy health insurance, the more expensive it will be.

If you join for the first time at age thirty-five, you pay an extra 2% of the gross policy cost for each year above the age of thirty-four that you didn't have health insurance. This additional charge is called a Lifetime Community Rating loading.

How do you find the best health-insurance policy for you?

1. Focus on your personal health needs

If you're young and healthy, you might be tempted to think you won't need health insurance. However, remember that accidents can happen to anyone at any age. A lower level of cover may be better than none at all.

If you plan to have children, look for a plan with good pre-natal, maternity, and post-natal care cover. Consider plans that are free for children if you have a young family.

If you're nearing retirement or aged over sixty-five, you'll want to check whether your plan covers things that may become important in older age. For example, some health insurance companies demand 'co-payments' of up to €2,000 for orthopaedic procedures, such as hip replacement.

If you have a lot of day-to-day medical expenses, you may need good coverage in that area. And if you want no surprises, consider a policy with little or no 'excess' payments. That's the amount you'll have to pay out-of-pocket before your insurance kicks in.

In all stages of life, it's crucial to review your health insurance regularly, as your needs can change.

2. Look at your budget and costs

It's important to consider how much you can afford to pay for your health insurance. Premiums can vary widely based on the level of coverage. You can considerably reduce the cost if you agree to pay a higher excess. This may be more suitable if you're young, healthy and have a good emergency fund.

3. Check out potential waiting periods with different providers

You may have to serve waiting periods of up to twenty-six weeks if you take out health insurance for the first time. You may also have a waiting period if it has been over thirteen weeks since you last held private health insurance. Also, you may not have cover for up to five years with a pre-existing condition if you take out health insurance for the first time.

Waiting periods also apply if you are switching policies – particularly upgrading to a policy with higher cover. Waits of up to two years for higher benefits may apply to patients with pre-existing conditions. Higher maternity benefits may take fifty-two weeks to kick in. Check each provider's stipulations.

4. Geography

What hospitals and clinics are close to you? If a private or public hospital is close, consider a policy that gives you suitable cover there. Is there a VHI Urgent Care clinic in your area or a Laya

Walk-in Urgent Care clinic? If you have young children involved in sports at the weekend, this may be an essential consideration for you.

Where does private health insurance fit in a financial plan?

Reading *Money Made Easy* from front to back, you will read about products of all shapes and sizes that can help your financial well-being.

I appreciate you may have to make some hard choices on which products you can afford. At times, you will also feel pressure to let policies go.

However, I always urge clients to have health insurance. As someone who has had his fair share of health knocks, private health insurance has significantly benefited me and my family.

Do I place health insurance above income protection, life or illness cover? No, I don't. Private health insurance is a complementary and necessary part of a financial protection plan.

If you ever need to drop a part of your protection plan, do so carefully. Cancelling life cover, critical-illness cover or income protection may result in you being unable to get the cover again. At least health insurance is always more accessible, and providers must give you cover.

If you're a business owner seeking health insurance for staff, it's best to engage a professional to review potential plans. I know several good health-insurance advice firms, and I'm happy to recommend them if anyone contacts me.

Never assume that your health-insurance policy covers you for every eventuality. They generally don't. Their plans, with varying excesses and different levels of cover, are often complex and over-engineered. This is not in the interests of the consumers.

As premiums tend to be in the thousands, not hundreds, it's vital to keep reviewing private health insurance every year as part of an effective financial plan.

What does 'protecting my estate' mean?

'My estate? What estate? I live in a three-bedroom semi-detached house in the suburbs.' That's the most common response when I broach this subject with older clients.

Yes, talking about 'protecting your estate' may sound very grand. Many of you will think protecting an estate is the preserve of the wealthy and those living in manor houses. Estate planning is simply insurance that protects your loved ones from overexposure to a stealth tax – inheritance tax.

Why do I need estate planning?

Since the 1990s, Ireland has seen a significant increase in personal wealth, predominantly through property ownership. Many people own valuable homes, second homes, farmland, holiday homes and even properties abroad.

In addition, thanks to the country's economic growth, household savings have increased to an estimated €150 billion sitting in deposits by 2023. We've also seen billions more invested in pension and retirement funds, a trend we've never seen before. Also, the modern Irish family is usually smaller, meaning larger inheritances for fewer children.

But what does this mean for you?

Imagine this – you've spent your whole life paying taxes

and, when you die, your loved ones face another 33% tax on *your* property and investments. It's important to note that spouses can inherit an estate tax free, but your children or other beneficiaries will likely face a large tax bill. Children can inherit up to €335,000 tax free, although this figure can change with each new budget or government. Children may be forced to sell the family home to meet the inheritance tax while dealing with your loss.

What are the different perceptions of estate planning?

With inheritance and estate planning, I come across two types of clients:

- One feels their children are inheriting enough, and their reaction is, 'Let them pay the tax.'
- The other says, 'I've paid enough tax during my working life. I'm not letting the Revenue Commissioners tax my assets again after I've passed away.'

Personally, I'm with the latter.

CLIENT CASE
PETER & SARAH, AGED 34 & 32

Peter and Sarah's surviving parent passed away. The siblings were left everything, including their mother's home in Dublin worth €700,000, a holiday home in the southeast valued at €200,000, a pension fund of €180,000 and savings of €70,000. The entire estate was valued at €1.15 million.

Peter and Sarah each inherited €335,000 tax free (a total of €670,000). This left a balance of €480,000, which was taxed at 33%. The tax bill was €158,400 that had to be paid within a year.

The value of their inheritance was tied up in property and funds that took time to encash. However, Revenue charged penalties and interest in the meantime, so an even larger tax bill had to be met.

Many would say Peter and Sarah were privileged to inherit so much, but others might say their parents already paid tax on all their income and assets. Inheritance tax can feel like the family's money is being taxed twice.

If Peter and Sarah's mother had looked into estate planning, she could have protected her family against this tax burden with a Section 72 insurance policy. Proper estate planning can reduce the impact of inheritance taxes and ensure wealth is passed on to future generations in the most efficient way possible.

What is a Section 72 policy?

A Section 72 insurance policy is a life-assurance policy designed to offset inheritance tax bills – unfortunately, I find very few clients have heard of it. The money from the policy can pay the inheritance tax or part of it, depending on the level of cover and the tax liability.

The proceeds of the policy are tax free under current Irish tax law. Section 72 insurance is about passing on wealth in the most tax-efficient way possible. After all, it's your hard-earned wealth; why not protect it for your loved ones?

CLIENT CASE
FIONN, AGED 43

I'm aware of several clients who stand to inherit a lot from their parents simply because of the value of their family homes, especially in parts of Dublin.

Fionn's parents are in their seventies. They are not wealthy but have a very valuable home in Dublin. Fionn loves where he grew up, and his dream is to return to the area. However, even though his parents are leaving him the house, he admits that he's unlikely to ever be able to afford it. Right now, the inheritance tax due would be €550,000.

Fionn is a latecomer to the property ladder and has bought outside Dublin. He is unlikely to have enough equity or value in his home to meet an inheritance tax bill of this size and more.

I hate to see large chunks of people's hard work being snatched away by the Revenue Commissioners. However, this reluctance to speak about financial issues is never so apparent as when I try to talk about estate planning. I told Fionn there are ways he and his parents can work together to eliminate or reduce his inheritance tax bill, but he would need to talk to his parents.

'I couldn't do that,' he said. 'No way am I talking to them about that.'

This is the reaction I get from most clients. I get it. Many people find it uncomfortable to discuss their own or their loved ones' mortality. Estate planning reminds us of the inevitable end of life, which can be difficult to confront.

And no one seems to want to talk about money.

But this failure to talk results in hundreds of thousands of unnecessary tax burdens on families. It's a crazy situation.

What is the protection gap for women?

Female readers need to be aware of the protection gap for women. (I discuss the pension gap for women in Section 7 (Pensions).)

A protection gap is the difference between the amount of insurance coverage you have and the amount you need. The protection gap is often more significant for women than men because of several factors:

- As a result of income inequality, women often end up with less life- and health-insurance coverage than men. It's outrageous, but women in the EU still earn 13% less per hour than men, which limits their ability to afford adequate insurance cover.
- Women usually live longer than men, which means they're more likely to encounter serious health issues or require long-term care. This compounds the protection gap issue because they lack insurance coverage to meet these needs.

- As primary caregivers in the family, women are often under-valued and underinsured. They shoulder more family concerns and take more time off work, reducing their earning power.
- The value of a woman's work and care in the household and family is significant, but this is often overlooked when it comes to protection insurance.
- An industry bias towards men also causes protection gaps. The majority in the financial industry are still men, which skews perspectives and policies. There needs to be an increasing awareness of women's unique insurance requirements. Women's insurance needs are not always the same as men's.

I have worked at promoting gender issues in my business, but the industry can still do better. We need more tailor-made insurance products for women. Critical-illness insurance, for example, could be tailored to cover diseases that disproportionately affect women, like certain types of cancer.

I can only say that the financial industry owes women an apology and must do better. If you're reading this and feel your bank, broker or wealth manager isn't addressing your concerns thoroughly, please contact me on social media. I can request that one of our excellent female financial planners carry out a complete review of your protection needs and tailor a plan that's more suited to your needs as a woman.

What is business protection?
Are you one of the 250,000 self-employed people or company shareholders in Ireland? You may have personal life insurance, a pension plan or an investment fund. As a self-employed

person, you also probably understand the importance of income protection, given your critical role in the business.

However, many in your position don't consider business protection, also known as shareholder-protection insurance. This insurance is crucial if you're one of several shareholders in a small-to-medium enterprise (SME).

Shareholder-protection policies provide financial security to shareholders of a business. These policies kick in when a business owner has a critical illness diagnosis or suffers a disability or death.

The insurance proceeds pay for the deceased business owner's shares. This helps to ensure the smooth transfer of ownership and control of the company. It also provides financial security for the late shareholder's family. Shareholder protection is often combined with legal agreements such as a buy–sell agreement. These policies can be tailored to the business and shareholders' specific requirements.

So why do you not have it already? The most likely reason is that your financial planner didn't suggest it – or if it was, the importance of business protection wasn't stressed.

Why do you need business protection?

Take Ben and Gerry, friends who started an ice-cream business, each owning a 50% share. After years of hard work, their business turns a profit and is valued at €2 million. They are amazed.

Then disaster strikes, and Ben dies suddenly. His wife and kids inherit his share of the company, valued at €1 million.

Even though they've never been involved in the business, they own half of it. Gerry is in a bind. He doesn't have €1 million to

221

buy them out, but Ben's wife needs the money from the business and wants to sell the company.

To avoid this situation, Ben and Gerry could have used insurance similar in structure and cost to personal life insurance. Had they put shareholder protection in place, several things would have happened upon Ben's death:

- Ben's shares would have been transferred to Gerry, making him the sole owner.
- A lump-sum equivalent to Ben's share value would be paid out to Ben's family.
- The contentious issue of Ben's family's potential involvement in the business would be removed.
- Gerry would be free to focus on the business, and Ben's wife could get on with her life.

This kind of planning brings peace of mind to business owners in a surprisingly cost-effective way. This plan can vary to suit partnerships and other business arrangements.

The final word on protection planning

Protection is a vital but often overlooked component of financial well-being that helps to make your financial plan bomb-proof. There's little point in focusing on pensions and investment strategies without considering the potential risks that could derail all your financial goals.

Financial-protection planning is about making your future income safe and secure. Dull and reliable can be positive qualities, especially in an unpredictable world.

We often underestimate our own value and that of our income, but protection planning brings these to the fore of your financial plan. As I've said, protection planning is the first line of defence. It is a robust shield to protect your family's future from catastrophic shock.

Our lives can change in a minute, and unexpected events can occur at any moment. By prioritising protection planning, you can sleep more easily, knowing you have a financial safety net if everything goes awry. I've seen how life circumstances can turn in an instant, so I'm passionate about the importance of protection planning.

Don't wait until it's too late. A protection plan is about taking control of your financial security. Your peace of mind, your financial well-being and the well-being of those you care about may depend on it.

Your 7-point action plan for financial protection

- Assess your needs and the risks that threaten your financial well-being. Assessing your needs will help you determine the best protection for you.

- Evaluate your current protection coverage and any current insurance policies or coverage you have in place. Analyse this cover and see where there may be gaps.

- Identify your priorities for protection cover. If you have young children, life insurance may be your priority. If you run your own business, income protection may be crucial.

- Create a budget and establish your limits for protection planning. Allocate your resources to your financial priorities.
- Seek a reliable financial planner with expertise in protection planning. They will help guide you through the multitude of insurance policies and guide you to the ones that meet your specific needs.
- Implement your protection plan when you've taken advice on the best policies for you. Ensure you have copies of all documents for your records.
- Prepare to review your plan in a few years – as your life circumstances change, so can your protection needs.

SECTION 6
MORTGAGES

As far as finance goes, there's nothing quite as emotive for people as buying a home. That's because getting a mortgage and buying a home isn't just a financial transaction, it's a deeply personal and emotional journey. It's also an emotional rollercoaster with twists, turns and stomach-churning loop-the-loops.

Buying a house represents one of the biggest decisions people make in their lives – particularly in Ireland, where we wrap so many of our dreams and aspirations into owning our own homes. As a financial planner, I've had the joy of accompanying many clients on this journey, and it never gets old.

However, I know securing a house will be a tall order for first-time buyers who are reading this. You are really in uncharted waters. With a property-shortage crisis, high prices and spiking interest rates, you face quite a challenge. And nothing will fix this in the short term.

If you've secured a mortgage in recent years, take a moment to pat yourself on the back. It's no small feat. It reflects your earning power, ability to save and determination to plant roots in your community.

If you're still struggling to get on the property ladder, keep going. Buying a house in a property shortage and climbing interest rates can feel like you're sailing into a headwind. But if you're determined, I believe securing a home is within your grasp.

This section aims to chart a steady course through choppy waters and, hopefully, help you reach your journey's end – your dream home.

What is a mortgage?

Remember this saying: 'You're not buying a house; you're buying a mortgage.' It's a reminder that your home actually belongs to the bank. It will only be yours when the loan is entirely paid off in twenty or thirty years.

Most homebuyers realise a mortgage is a long-term financial obligation that will last several decades. However, they always don't grasp that, until it's paid off, they own the mortgage rather than the house itself.

A mortgage is a legal agreement to loan you money to buy a property. You slowly pay back the loan plus interest, usually over several decades. As you pay back money, you own a bigger and bigger share or 'equity' in the house.

But if you can't keep up with your payments, the lender may reclaim ownership of the property. The house remains the bank's collateral until you fully repay the mortgage.

Why do we need a mortgage?

Unfortunately, many of us can't afford to buy a property outright, whether it's a country cottage with a rose garden or a comfortable semi-detached in the suburbs.

That's where a mortgage comes in. It enables you to become a homeowner by breaking down the cost into manageable monthly payments that you make over many years (usually twenty to thirty-five years). As time passes and you continue to make your mortgage payments, you gain more and more ownership of your home.

Why are mortgage rates so important?

The price of your house is undoubtedly a critical factor for your finances. However, the mortgage attached to it can significantly influence your overall costs. The mortgage's terms – including the interest rates, the duration and other fees or charges – really impact how much you pay over time. By the time you pay off your loan, you could pay the original property's cost several times, especially if the interest rates rise enough.

Let's take the case of two friends, Anna and Ciara, as an example.

Anna took out a €350,000 mortgage over thirty years in

January 2022, with a 2.5% fixed rate. Over the thirty years, Anna will pay €147,852 in interest. The total cost of Anna's mortgage is €497,852.

Fast forward two years to January 2024, and Ciara also takes out a mortgage of €350,000 over thirty years. However, bank interest rates have risen in the intervening two years, and Anna's 2.5% rate is gone. Ciara's mortgage rate is 4.5%. Over the 30 years, she will pay €288,423. That's an additional €140,571 in interest. The total cost of Ciara's mortgage is €638,423.

That's the impact of a small interest-rate rise on the money you pay for your house.

Why is it important to learn about mortgage rates of interest?

A mortgage is probably your largest financial commitment, so it's important to understand your interest rate to see if you can reduce this outgoing. Yet, I've found that many homebuyers don't know how interest works on a mortgage. They don't know their balance, the type of mortgage they have, its term or when their fixed rate changes.

They also don't know how or when to switch mortgage providers. They have no concept of the money that it will save them.

The past ten years have distorted our view on mortgages and interest rates. Nobody paid much interest because rates were low and stable. They were affordable. Interest rates from the European Central Bank (ECB) were at 0%. Since early 2022, that has changed, and rates have been on the rise.

As you can see from the example of Anna and Ciara above,

a slight interest rate increase of 2% makes a vast difference on your bottom line. Ciara pays €140,571 more than her friend because her interest rate rose by 2%. Ask yourself how long it would take to save that amount from your take-home pay.

Why should I use a financial planner?

If the mortgage market is a maze, your financial planner is the sure-footed guide to lead you through the home-buying trail. They have the maps, and understand the terrain and all the shortcuts to help you reach your destination – house keys. These professionals can really take the guesswork out of the mortgage process and guide you towards the right decision.

But what exactly do they do, and when is it the right time to reach out to them? Let's discuss.

The mortgage broker or financial planner is a matchmaker between you and potential lenders. They are an intermediary between you and the banks, and they try to find the best lender and mortgage product to match your needs. They'll assess your financial status and then use their expertise to recommend the best mortgage deals.

You can, of course, go through the mortgage application process yourself. Many people do. However, using a financial planner can bring several potential advantages:

- They start by assessing your financial situation and chances of getting a mortgage. As a result, they can advise on how to present your financial situation to the bank to increase your chances of approval.

- A financial planner takes a more holistic view of your finances to review your financial situation. They will also advise you if you're wasting your time applying now and will tell you what changes you need to make before you apply for a mortgage.
- Using a planner saves you time and energy because they do the legwork of research and comparisons for you. They thoroughly understand the mortgage market and can often access deals and rates you wouldn't find by yourself. A planner can walk you through more complicated parts of the mortgage process and the paperwork.
- They have no ties or loyalty to any one lender. A broker makes money by analysing the market and playing lenders off one another. He also gets paid the same commission rate from every bank, so he has no favourites.

More and more people are using mortgage brokers today. In 2013, 85% of people applying for a mortgage went to their banks – only 15% used a mortgage broker. By 2023, the split was 50% each. A mortgage involves so much money that if you make the wrong decision, it can cost not only thousands but hundreds of thousands. Research the market, get familiar with the products and then take professional, independent advice.

At what stage do I see a financial planner?
If you're a first-time buyer or haven't navigated the mortgage process for a while, I recommend seeing one sooner rather than later. Meeting a planner before house-hunting can help you prepare your finances for a mortgage application.

Preparation can take time. It might take six months or more before your finances and bank statements are looking their best and ready for making an application.

Even if you're just considering buying a house, it's worth seeing a planner to set you on the right path.

How do banks fund mortgages?

Banking is funded in two different ways.

- Some people seem to think the bank keeps their savings deposits in some vast vault. 'Hey, it's not in the safe?' No, but it's still safe. The government has guaranteed deposits of up to €100,000, and your money may even earn a small amount of interest.

  However, your savings are gone. The bank has put them out to work. This clever business model has been in use since ancient times. The bank offers low or no interest rates to you for your money. Then, it loans it to your neighbour with 9% interest on a personal loan or 4% on a mortgage.

- Banks also buy money 'wholesale' from the European Central Bank (ECB). The banks buy the ECB's money at an interest rate of, say, 4.5% and then they add a profit margin when they loan it out to us. The ECB interest rates were 0% for six years, so Irish banks made an enormous margin on mortgages up to 2022.

Who are the mortgage lenders in Ireland?

When I started my career in finance, there were about sixteen lenders in Ireland, many offering 100% mortgages.

However, the high-street mortgage market shrank dramatically during the property crash after 2008. Several banks, including Bank of Scotland, Anglo-Irish Bank, Irish Nationwide Building Society, Ulster Bank, ACC, Danske Bank and KBC have exited retail banking.

Subprime lenders – Stepstone, Springboard, GE Money and Start Mortgages – who offered loans to higher-risk borrowers are no longer on the mortgage market.

Three non-bank lenders – Avant Money, ICS Mortgages and Finance Ireland – opened for business from 2016 and shook up the high-street lenders. They made the mortgage market a more competitive environment for a while.

However, the interest rate rises have affected the alternative lenders more than the mainstream banks. The non-bank lenders cannot access cheap or free money from Irish savers. Avant Money, which is funded by Bankinter (one of Europe's biggest banks), ICS Mortgages and Finance Ireland must buy their money wholesale from the ECB.

Not surprisingly, Central Bank data in 2023 revealed that alternative lenders' variable mortgage rates are now higher on average than those of mainstream banks.

As of the end of 2023, the Irish mortgage lenders are:
- The giants of Irish banking – AIB, Bank of Ireland, Permanent TSB and EBS (a subsidiary of AIB).
- Haven, a broker-only lender and part of the AIB Group.
- The three non-bank lenders – Avant Money, ICS Mortgages and Finance Ireland – offer mortgages, albeit at less competitive rates than previously.
- Credit unions, some of which also offer mortgages. Although

expensive in the past, over the past twelve months their rates have become more competitive compared to a tracker or high fixed-rate mortgage in the bank.

- MoCo, a new entrant to the market that has begun testing their offering via four brokers.

There has been talk about An Post entering the market, but nothing has come of this so far.

What does the European Central Bank have to do with my mortgage?

Let's start with a sense of how the macro-banking environment works. The European Central Bank (ECB) in Frankfurt decides Ireland's monetary policy and interest rates. Yes, we have a say and representatives there, including the Central Bank of Ireland governor, Gabriel Makhlouf. Philip Lane of Trinity College is the ECB's chief economist.

The ECB states its primary aim is to preserve the euro's purchasing power. It does this by ensuring that inflation – the rate at which the overall prices for goods and services change over time – remains low, stable and predictable. It aims to control inflation at 2%. I think we all agree its inflation-control efforts haven't been going particularly well for the past two years.

Why 2%?

Businesses like predictability too. In fact, inflation control is good for all of us, even though constantly rising interest rates aren't great for our wallets.

Our banks' interest rates are based on the ECB's rates.

Unfortunately, the ECB hiked rates ten times between 2022 and 2023 as rates rose from 0% to 4.5% by the end of 2023.

Inflation in the eurozone spiked because of the Ukraine war, rising energy prices and disrupted supply chains since COVID-19. Also, 'protectionism' is a growing mindset. Countries are restricting international trade to benefit domestic industries. Rising wages because of workforce changes since COVID-19 are not helping either. Employers struggle to attract and keep workers in an era that spawned the terms the 'Big Quit', the 'Great Resignation' and the 'Quiet Quitting'.

Despite the ECB's efforts to slow down the economy with interest rate charges, inflation remains stubbornly high.

What do European Central Bank interest-rate hikes mean for Irish mortgages?

All ECB interest-rate hikes have been reflected in the monthly repayments for tracker-rate mortgages (see p240). As a result, Ireland's 240,000 tracker mortgage holders have been feeling the burn of much higher repayments for the past year.

The banks have been slower to raise the variable and fixed rates because they have used savers' money to subsidise these mortgages. However, criticism of the banks for not paying interest on savings may lead to higher variable and fixed mortgage rates.

Interest rate hikes affect everyone with variable mortgage rates and those with fixed-rate mortgages coming to the end of agreed terms. First-time buyers trying to climb onto the property ladder also face higher interest rates. We are looking at a whole new and more expensive mortgage reality.

The bad news is that experts expect rates to stay at these levels for the foreseeable future as underlying inflation is proving hard to tackle.

What is a fixed rate, standard variable rate or tracker mortgage?

You plan to buy a house and hear people throwing around terms like 'tracker', 'variable rate' and 'fixed rate'. What are they talking about – and which one is right for you?

What is a fixed-rate mortgage?

A fixed-rate mortgage is easy to understand. With this type, the interest rate stays the same for a set period, usually between one and ten years, but sometimes longer. In Central Europe, it's common to fix your mortgage for twenty-five years or more and the non-bank lenders in Ireland recently introduced fixed rates of thirty years in Ireland. (See my favourite one below.)

The major advantage of a fixed rate term is that you know what your monthly repayments are for the entire term as you will have no rate increases. You have no surprises. Obviously, if interest rates fall, you may have buyer's remorse because you end up paying more than everyone on a variable rate; but if interest rates rise, you pay less than everyone else and can feel smug.

From a financial-planning perspective, taking professional advice when choosing your rate is important.

During 2022, I pleaded with everyone – especially those on trackers and those coming off fixed-term rates – to move to a long-term fixed rate. At the time, Finance Ireland offered a twenty-five-year rate of 2.65%. Yes, in 2022, you could have fixed your mortgage for twenty-five years at that rate. Other lenders offered shorter fixed rates at 2.5%. The best fixed rate in 2024 will likely be at least 5%.

As *Money Made Easy* goes to print, Finance Ireland no longer offers fixed rates over five years. And their five-year fixed rate is between 6% and 6.45%, depending on your loan-to-value (LTV).

The loan-to-value ratio refers to the proportion of your property that's mortgaged versus your equity in it. This means if your house value is €300,000, and you make a 10% deposit of €30,000 on the property, the LTV is 90%.

Finance Ireland is not a high-street bank or well-known lender, and they only promote their mortgages through the network of brokers. This is one example of why it's best to consult a mortgage broker when considering a mortgage. You'll have a far wider range of mortgage options than walking into one bank.

While fixed rates offer stability and peace of mind, they lack flexibility. Penalties can be charged if you move to a different lender or remortgage during the term. Banks lifted some of these restrictions as interest rates increased over the past two years. If you fixed recently, you're unlikely to face a penalty for securing another rate with an existing provider or switching to another bank. Check with your bank to see if you face a penalty for switching. If not, it may be worth shopping around.

When you come to the end of a fixed-rate term, banks will offer you the option of a variable-rate mortgage or to fix again.

If you're about to come off a fixed-rate mortgage, be proactive. Seek a mortgage broker to see if switching is an option or to seize the best rates on the market.

Do not sleepwalk into a decision that could cost you thousands a year.

My favourite fixed-rate mortgage right now

At the time *Money Made Easy* is going to print, one of my favourite lenders and rates on the market is Avant Money's One Mortgage.

It enables clients to fix for the whole term of their mortgage, and they fix the rate at 3.9% to 4.1% depending on loan-to-value.

This mortgage does everything most don't do but should:

- It offers flexibility to borrowers to overpay and clear their mortgage early; you can overpay 10% of the outstanding balance in any given year. So, if your mortgage is €280,000 you can overpay €28,000 in that year without facing a penalty (maximum of two lump sum payments per year).

  Bank of Ireland, in comparison, only allows you to overpay 10% of your mortgage repayment. If your mortgage repayment is €1,500 per month, you can only overpay by €150 per month or €1,800 a year.

- Avant Money's One Mortgage will waive the breakage fee on the mortgage should you wish to move home during the fixed term, providing you take the new mortgage with Avant.

For example, John and Mary have a mortgage with Avant for €200,000, fixed at 3.9% with fifteen years remaining. Let's say, in a few years they want to move home and need a new mortgage of €300,000. In normal circumstances the lender would apply a penalty for breaking the loan, however if John and Mary borrow the mortgage amount from Avant they will waive the penalty. Avant will allow them to move their €200,000 mortgage on the existing house to the new property, which means they only have to borrow an additional €100,000 from Avant.

If rates increased since they took out their first loan, this is good news for John and Mary. Obviously, terms and conditions apply, but the point is you can find great flexibility in fixed-rate contracts these days. Talk to a good mortgage broker.

What is a standard variable-rate mortgage?
This mortgage is like a rollercoaster because, as 'variable' suggests, the interest rate can go up or down.

This means your monthly payments can vary over time. Your lender decides the standard variable rate (SVR), not the European Central Bank (ECB), but general economic conditions influence it. If the ECB rates are high, the lender's rates may follow. However, mainstream Irish banks' interest rates are now more closely linked to their deposit rates than the ECB. The banks that pay more interest on savings deposits charge more for their variable-rate mortgages and vice versa.

However, the rates charged will also depend on the bank's profit margins and the level of competition in the market. Anyone on a variable-rate mortgage may also benefit from falling ECB interest rates, but that's unlikely in the current market.

Flexibility is the primary appeal of a variable-rate mortgage. You needn't worry about penalties if you switch, move to a fixed rate or wish to increase your monthly repayments because of a windfall or a better salary. I usually recommend variable rates if a client plans to significantly reduce their mortgage or clear it with a lump sum in the near future.

Variable or fixed – which is better?

People ask us if they should fix or stick with a variable. In 2022, I advised everyone who'd listen to move to fixed-rate mortgages before the interest rates rose. I still recommend fixing and fixing for the long term for readers reading *Money Made Easy* in early 2024. Please see 'Where is the mortgage market going in 2024?' near the end of this section for more details.

Sometimes, the choice of variable or fixed comes down to preference.

If you like to budget, prefer stability and want to know exactly what your payments will be, a fixed rate is a good choice. But if you're willing to take the risk that rates could go down and want to potentially pay less, a standard variable-rate mortgage might be right for you. Each type of mortgage has its pros and cons.

- Are you conservative by nature? Do you value stability above all else?
  Answer: Move to a fixed rate.
- Do you think you'll pay off your mortgage early, anyway?
  Answer: Stay on a variable rate.
- Do you plan to switch your mortgage soon?
  Answer: Stay on the variable rate until you weigh up your options.
- Do you plan to move home soon?
  Answer: Stay on a variable or a flexible fixed rate to avoid any penalties.

My advice is to go to a mortgage broker or financial planner if you have questions about a mortgage. Making a wrong decision with your mortgage can be an expensive mistake.

Tracker mortgages

Imagine a hound faithfully following the trail of the European Central Bank (ECB) lending rate. That's what the tracker mortgage does. Your mortgage interest rate is 'tracking' the ECB's rate. An example of a tracker mortgage in action is AIB or Bank of Ireland offering a deal such as 'ECB rate plus 1%'.

That means your interest rate is 1% when the ECB rate is 0% - and it was 0% for six years.

Trackers were inexpensive loans for years as the ECB rates remained historically low. They became popular during the Celtic Tiger days of the early 2000s when the economy boomed. However, trackers became less profitable after the global financial crisis in 2008, and most banks stopped offering them to new customers.

However, they are no longer inexpensive. By the end of 2023, the ECB rate was 4.5%, which meant AIB or Bank of Ireland's standard tracker rate was 5.5%. (ECB rate at 4.5% plus 1%.) Others are paying as high as 6.45% depending on their deal.

What do I do with a tracker mortgage now?

I get a lot of enquiries about whether tracker mortgage holders should switch to another mortgage product. In Ireland, we have around 240,000 tracker mortgages. These loans are at least fifteen years old because most banks stopped offering them in 2008. It means people have, on average, ten to fifteen years left on a reduced mortgage.

With rates soaring in 2023, it's little wonder that many people are feeling the pressure financially. Anyone with a tracker mortgage of 1% with €225,000 outstanding and fifteen years remaining went from paying around €1,380 a month to €1,780 a month.

It means their mortgage repayments have increased by €4,800 a year. This amounts to spending an extra €7,000 to €9,000 of their gross salary on their mortgage.

Consider switching if you have a significant tracker balance and are under financial pressure. If the sustained interest rates (or potential for further increases) are a concern, switching or going to a fixed rate may be an option.

How much can I borrow?
The Central Bank controls the amount you can borrow. They introduced tight mortgage rules in 2015 to avoid a repeat of the free-for-all during the Celtic Tiger era before 2008. They also set the deposit you need to buy a house.

1. Loan-to-income limit
As a first-time borrower, you can borrow up to four times your gross income since January 2023.

Banks calculate income by taking your basic salary plus 50% of your average bonus and other non-guaranteed income. This varies from lender to lender with some lenders taking more than 50% into account. So, for example, a first-time buyer couple with a combined income of €100,000 can borrow up to a maximum of €400,000.

However, this is the maximum you may borrow. Banks may reduce your loan amount if you have outgoings on personal loans and commitments, such as childcare.

Second-time buyers can borrow up to three and a half times their gross income. So, for example, a second-time buyer with an income of €100,000 can borrow up to a maximum of €350,000.

2. Loan-to-value ratio

Loan-to-value refers to the percentage of the property's value you can borrow. Under these rules, first- and second-time buyers can borrow up to 90% of the house's purchase price. That means you need a minimum of 10% deposit.

If you want to buy a €400,000 home, you will need a deposit of €40,000 because you can only borrow a maximum of €360,000.

Buy-to-let investors can only borrow a maximum of 70% of the house's purchase price, so they need a minimum deposit of 30%.

Is there any wiggle room with borrowing limits?

Yes, lenders have a certain amount of what's called 'exemptions' for certain applicants.

In any year, 15% of first-time buyers can seek to borrow up to four and a half times their income. The same exemption is possible for second-time buyers, and 10% of buy-to-let-investors can also borrow above the limits, although the bank's lending policy usually exempts buy-to-let investors doing this. Just because the Central Bank allows it, doesn't mean the bank has to allow it.

You can qualify for an exemption if your credit report is excellent and the banks approve your application. However, lenders can use up these quotas in the first few months of the year, so they're often unavailable.

What is a credit report?

Ireland doesn't have an agency that gives credit ratings, like in the UK or the US. Instead, the Central Bank established the Central Credit Register (CCR), which issues a credit 'report' rather than a credit score or rating. The CCR doesn't decide on granting or refusing credit. Neither does it produce a credit score or a credit rating. The CCR includes factual details about repayments, both good (when you make a payment) and bad (when you fail to pay).

Does a credit report matter? Yes, it does – it matters even when you already have a mortgage. Because a good credit report gives you the best opportunity to get credit in the future.

The CCR keeps credit information on all loans of €500 or higher and provides these reports to potential lenders. Your report shows information on all loans and holds all payment details for five years after you make the last payment. The details include personal loans, credit union loans, credit cards, overdrafts, mortgages, business loans, car finance and hire purchases.

When you fill out your mortgage application or form for any loan, the lender checks your credit history. Even though the CCR holds information for five years, lenders will only see the previous two years of your credit report when they request a copy. The report helps the lenders decide whether to give you a loan.

Can I get a copy of my credit report?

You can get access to your credit report. Go to www.central creditregister.ie to request a free copy of your report. You must provide photo ID, proof of address and proof of your PPSN. As well as your credit details, you will see the lenders who have checked your report in the past five years. They leave a 'footprint' showing when they saw your report and why. You can find 'footprints' at the bottom of your credit report.

Request the CCR to change the data on your report if you think it's incomplete, inaccurate or out of date.

How do I get a good credit report?

If negative information appears on your CCR report, you are seen as a bad risk for lenders. To avoid this, do the following.

- Only borrow what you can afford so you repay the amount on time and in full. A track record of repaying loans is reassuring for lenders.
- If payment becomes an issue, talk to your lender before you miss any payments and agree to a way forward. However, your lender must report alternative repayment arrangements to the CCR.
- If you receive a negative note on your report, you can also insert an explanatory statement on your credit report – up to two hundred words on why you missed a payment. This can make a vital difference when a lender is reviewing your report.
- Sometimes, people make mistakes and your credit report is incorrect. Check your report before you begin the application process and make sure everything is accurate. As a borrower,

you can contact the CCR and request that they remove incorrect information from your credit report.

- Remember, even though a bad loan can last up to five years on the CCR, lenders will only see the previous two years of your credit report when they request a copy. You may have to wait two years for the negative information to disappear before making a mortgage application.
- Remember, too, the credit record is only one of several factors considered when assessing any loan application.
- No, taking out a loan to demonstrate good loan-servicing capacity is not a good idea. Paying interest when you don't have to is not sound financial planning.

How do I get a mortgage and buy a house?

Below is a crash course on the fairy-tale version of getting a mortgage and buying a house.

- You examine your finances. This includes your savings, income, regular expenses and any debts you owe. All these factors will influence how big a mortgage you can afford.
- You clean up your act – clear your loans, save like crazy and erase every trace of betting apps from your accounts if you have them.
- You research everything. (You're making a great start by reading this book.) Not all mortgages or banks are the same; they can have different interest rates, and terms and conditions.
- Go to a lender for full 'approval in principle' (AIP). Better still, get a broker or financial planner to apply for your

approval. You fill out many forms, or the broker does, and the bank (or banks) assesses your financial situation and tells you the amount they'll lend you.

- Armed with your pre-approval, you can now start house hunting for your dream home.
- Found the perfect place? Make an offer.
- When it's accepted, you'll return to your lender or broker to get your final loan offer. The house must be valued for the bank. The bank issues you with a final offer – including conditions, such as mortgage protection and home insurance.
- Your solicitor will check the deeds and the contracts for the property. The paperwork is signed, the Ts are crossed, and the Is are dotted. The bank transfers your loan amount to your solicitor.
- Yay! You get the keys to your first home.

What's the reality of getting a mortgage and buying a house?

So, you want the real story of getting a mortgage and buying your first house?

The entire process can be one of the most emotional, tear-stained, frustrating and stressful periods you'll ever experience.

Buying a house was never easy, but the competition for a home in a property-shortage crisis makes it a real ordeal now. You race to multiple viewings, make bids on properties, wait forever for replies and complete vast reams of paperwork – all while holding down a job. The administration is huge, chasing solicitors is stressful and waiting for survey results is nail-biting. Even when your offer is accepted, the fear of the sale falling through keeps many home buyers awake at night.

Buckle up – this is not for the faint-hearted.

How does the first-time buyer get a mortgage?

The deposit
The first hurdle for the first-time buyer is to get the 10% deposit together – but 10% of what? It's challenging when you don't know what amount to save.

Start with your income and that of your partner, if any. The maximum you can hope for is four times your combined salary. Then, research the property market in your desired location. Can you find properties in this area in your price range?

When you estimate the property price, you can calculate 10%. For example, if your estimated property price is €300,000, the 10% deposit would be €30,000.

Factor in the fact you may end up in a bidding war. If you want to buy a place with an asking price of €300,000, you may need to add an extra 10% to your budget. Better still, subtract 10% and aim for a price closer to €270,000, to allow for that potential escalation in price.

The savings strategy
When you know the deposit amount, you can set a savings goal and start saving systematically. Determine a timeframe within which you want to save the deposit and divide the total amount

by the number of months or years you have. This will help you determine how much you need to save each month.

Identify areas where you can reduce expenses and allocate more funds towards your savings goal. All lenders will allow you to be gifted money by a family member. They ask that you provide a letter confirming the gift and the nature of your relationship with the donor. You may receive a gift up to the value of €3,000 from *any* person in a calendar year without paying Capital Acquisitions Tax (CAT). This means you may take a gift from several people in the same calendar year. A couple with four generous parents can receive €12,000 without paying tax.

Consider additional costs associated with buying a property, such as legal fees, stamp duty and inspection costs.

The credit report
Make sure your credit report is squeaky clean (see above). Pay down debts if you can, and always pay your bills on time. If there are any errors in your report, get them fixed.

The big account clean-up
Lenders are looking to see stable income and savings. If you are a sole trader, you must show two years of full accounts so they can assess a pattern of income.

They will look back on at least six months into all your statements and pull down your credit report. As they assess you, they will find all your accounts, from Revolut to that old post office account. Gambling online is a red flag to the banks. Yes, they want a goody-two-shoes and that's how you must present yourself.

Make sure you have a visible debit for your monthly rent and all your big payments. The banks want a paper trail. Don't have any significant cash disappearing from your accounts.

If you were in Australia or Canada for a few years and left a trail of debts, those debts will catch up with you too, probably during this process.

The lender's business is selling money. They want to give that money to you, but you must look like a safe bet. They need to see a cushion of cash still in your account at the end of the month. This leftover cash is net disposable income (NDI).

This will tell them your ability to withstand the financial stress of potential increases in interest rates. (A concept that was well-tested in 2022.)

The perfect job

The banks love reliable, pensionable careers, such as civil servants, and certain well-paid professions. However, demonstrating a strong ability for financial planning and budgeting is just as important.

Don't even think of switching careers during the process. The banks will regard the first six months in a new job as a probationary period. If you change jobs, you'll have to suspend the house-hunting process for six months before you look like a secure bet in the eyes of the lender.

The A-team

Buying a house takes a village … well, not really. But this is when you need to engage with a financial planner or mortgage broker. You also need to think about a solicitor to handle the conveyancing of a property from the seller to you.

The matchmaker

You'll certainly need a mortgage broker to buy anything out of the ordinary. Some lenders are more receptive to self-builds, for example. Others focus on urban-area lending. You'll find another couple are more favourably disposed towards buy-to-let mortgages. Remember, a bank can only offer you their own products. A mortgage broker can offer you everything on the market.

Approval in principle

When your savings are on track and your account statements are sparkling, it's time to get mortgage approval in principle (AIP). This is a conditional approval from a bank stating how much they will lend you. It's not a guarantee, but it'll show sellers you're a serious buyer.

Keep calm and carry on

Above all, take a deep breath and don't take this process personally. You are a kite in the wind in the property and lending market. Dozens of variables must align to get your mortgage approved and secure a property.

Be patient, realistic and disciplined, and you will get there.

Is it easier for second-time buyers to buy a house?

Well, you'd think a second time around on this merry-go-round would be much easier, wouldn't you? But 'movers' can only borrow three and a half times their gross income, which hardly seems fair, seeing that you have already proven your ability to find a mortgage.

However, the Central Bank of Ireland considers second-time buyers riskier bets than new buyers because they are generally older and less likely to have future wage increases. It's harsh but true.

The good news is that the deposit requirement was reduced in January 2023 from a previous demand of 20% to 10%. Also, a second-time buyer should not find the process as daunting as it is for the newbies.

Well, it shouldn't be, but it usually is. This time around, you'll often find yourself in a chain sale. You'll be selling your home to fund your property purchase. And that seller is also selling to move to another property. And the guy who wants to buy your property is waiting for the sale of his property to go through ...

You'll be in the centre of many moving variables, and everything is out of your control, including solicitors, banks, estate agents, the house sale and your house purchase. (See 'Keep calm and carry on' on the previous page.)

How do I switch mortgages?

The great switch occurred between 2021 and 2022 as some people rushed to avail of low fixed rates. KBC and Ulster Bank quit the mortgage market here, forcing other homeowners to switch. This was a positive move, as many are on better interest rates than previously. And they're certainly on better rates now than anyone who didn't fix their rates.

The switching market is not competitive in 2024, but it's still worth doing in some instances.

By switching your mortgage and reducing your interest rate,

you can reduce your monthly payments or mortgage term. This can result in tens of thousands of savings over the life of your mortgage.

Also note that you cannot switch your mortgage to a more sustainable rate if you are in arrears. Unfortunately, you are known in the business as a 'mortgage prisoner'.

The first step to switching is getting an up-to-date valuation of your property. You'll also need a solicitor to do the legal work. Thankfully, the legal services will not be as expensive as the initial purchase. The average legal fees cost around €1,500 and valuation fees cost about €160. However, many lenders offer 'switcher packages' to cover the cost of your legal and valuation fees.

CLIENT CASE
MARK & AISHLING, AGED 36

This couple saw me discuss mortgage interest rates on Virgin Media's *Weekend AM* in early 2022. I was busy urging people to fix their rates before they rose, and they heeded my advice and made an appointment to see me.

When I met them, they had a three-bed, semi-detached home valued at €450,000. Their mortgage was €333,000, on a variable rate of 3.8% over a twenty-six-year term. Their repayments were €1,700 per month.

After a consultation, I advised the clients to switch their mortgage to Finance Ireland and secured a rate of 2.9% for a reduced term of twenty years. This made repayments €1,830, just over €100 per month more expensive, but it reduced the mortgage term from twenty-six to twenty years.

The interest cost on this mortgage is €106,000, meaning the couple will pay back €439,244 over twenty years.

Looking back now, Mark and Aishling have one of the cheapest mortgage interest rates in the Irish market and most likely will do so for the next nineteen years.

If they had come to me at the end of 2023, the best rate available for the same term was 4.1%, an increase of 1.2% but still significant. The couple's repayment would have been €2,035 per month (€205 more expensive). And the interest costs over the twenty years would have jumped from €106,000 to €155,521. They would have had to pay out an extra €49,521.

The paperwork involves an initial submission to the lender, which can be done with your bank of choice. However, having it prepared by a mortgage broker or financial planner is better. Then you'll require documents and statements to verify your information. The process takes around six weeks, and a mortgage broker or financial planner will manage most of this for you.

Use this time to review your mortgage-protection policy and assess your overall protection needs. Since you bought the home, you may have had kids, got married or had changes in salary.

What is a buy-to-let mortgage?

A buy-to-let mortgage is for people looking to purchase a property to rent out to others. We can also describe it as a buy-to-rent or a residential investment property (RIP) mortgage. Property is a popular investment option and the ability to cover the mortgage while making a steady income attracts investors.

Buying a residential property essentially makes you a landlord. The market is not friendly to landlords right now, so I always urge clients to consider carefully before becoming amateur property tycoons. Lenders consider buy-to-let mortgages higher risk than residential mortgages. They fear you may experience problems with rent collection or endure periods where the property is empty. As a result, you need a minimum 30% deposit and may borrow up to 70% of the property's value.

However, I advise clients not to invest in a property unless they have at least a 50% deposit. As I've said in Section 3 (Saving and Investing), three hands are out for your rental income in a property investment. The first hand to be filled is the Revenue Commissioners, then the bank and, finally, you. The smaller the mortgage, the more likely you will see some rental income.

I've come across people who forget about the Revenue Commissioners when making calculations on their investment. Rent is income and is subject to tax. I highly recommend getting independent financial planning and tax advice before considering the purchase of an investment property.

Buy-to-let mortgages are usually different from a standard mortgage for a residential property. The interest rates are higher for a start. However, banks can provide these mortgages on an interest-only basis. This means your monthly repayments pay off your interest but not the capital owed on the property.

This is an advantage in the short term, as you'll have more cash available. However, the full capital of the loan will have to be repaid at the end of the mortgage term, so you'll need to have a solid plan. This means selling the property, using savings made during the mortgage term or refinancing with another mortgage. If the property prices fall during the mortgage term, you risk not making enough from the sale to cover the capital cost of the property.

You can, of course, use the traditional repayment model and pay a standard loan on capital and interest for your buy-to-let. This option is best, as you'll have paid off the loan at the end of the mortgage term. You will own the property and have a passive income. The rental income will only be shared between you and the Revenue Commissioners when the mortgage is paid off.

I see a lot of accidental landlords who went into negative equity during the property crash after 2008. They have stressful stories to tell. Unless you have a decent upfront cash sum to invest and a genuine interest in being a landlord, I would reconsider this route as the best way to accumulate wealth.

Green mortgages

Green mortgages are a growing trend in Ireland among the socially conscious – and those looking for the best mortgage deal. Environmental, social and governance (ESG) investing is becoming more popular. Of course, some companies are accused of 'greenwashing' their credentials. However, moving towards energy-efficient homes makes sense with rising utility costs.

So, what is a green mortgage? This mortgage offers a lower interest rate for people buying more energy-efficient homes. To qualify, you must buy a new or second-hand home with a Building Energy Rating (BER) of B3 or higher. Several lenders offer green mortgages, which provide slightly cheaper fixed-rate mortgages.

The discounts available are around 0.35%, which seems small but can amount to hundreds every year of the mortgage term.

Are green mortgages worth considering?

Homes with a higher BER are more expensive to begin with, but if you want an energy-efficient home, a green mortgage may be the way to go. All homes built since 2019 have to be A2-rated.

If you upgrade the BER on your existing house and reach B3 standard or higher, it may make sense to consider switching to a green mortgage. However, these mortgages are all fixed – there is no variable green mortgage. They are usually short-term fixed rates too, which may not be ideal if you are looking for predictability in your budget.

I'd always urge that you get good independent mortgage advice before deciding.

What is a self-build mortgage?

The dream of building your own home is popular among people in rural areas. Some lenders are specialists in this space, while others don't go near self-builds as a matter of policy. Non-traditional lenders have generally shied away from self-builds.

A self-build mortgage works differently from buying a ready-built house in an urban area.

- If you're lucky enough to own or be gifted the site, you may not need a deposit as the site is part of the completed house value. However, the lender will always seek a 10% cash contingency plan. Banks know most projects will exceed the estimated building cost, and the last thing they want is their finance invested in an unfinished house because you ran out of money.

- With a self-build mortgage, you will draw down the money according to set stages in the construction. You only pay interest on the amount you've drawn down, not the total loan amount. It's often a complicated process as life doesn't go that smoothly, and neither does construction. Project coordination, builders, delayed supplies and staggered timelines are all part of the mix. A final inspection is needed before final funds are drawn down.

- One of the biggest mistakes I see people making when building their own house is to start work before getting the mortgage. I see clients who might have family in the building trade and start the foundations and drainage and then look for the mortgage. This is a red light for a bank as they want an architect or surveyor to sign off on each stage of the self-build process. If you've done a solo run on the first stage of the house, it may mean the bank won't offer the mortgage.

Self-building is more complicated than the traditional house purchase. Please go in with your eyes open if you are considering this as an option.

What extra costs are there besides the mortgage?

- Your closing fees will include stamp duty, which is 1% of your purchase value up to €1 million; 2% is due on the balance of any property that costs over €1 million.
- Legal fees for conveyancing vary but are rarely below €2,000.
- The pre-purchase inspection or house survey costs around €500–€750 for a modest-sized house or apartment in Dublin, Cork or Galway.
- Home insurance is mandatory.
- Mortgage protection is mandatory and must be set up before the mortgage. This life policy pays out to repay your loan to the bank should you die.
- Don't be too precious with furniture and decorating. How do you eat an elephant? One chunk at a time. First, get a couple of main rooms sorted: a living room, kitchen and main bedroom. Worry about the garden and all the rest another time. Contrary to what Instagram tells you, you don't need a perfect show home. It's yours for life. Take your time. Buy well and buy once. You have time on your side.
- Avoid buy-now-pay-later options when setting up your first home. You already have a big debt with a mortgage. You don't need to accumulate smaller short-term debts just to furnish the house. The last thing you want is to start your new home journey with extra financial pressure.

Government help schemes for buying a home

The government has introduced several schemes to help people who are wanting to climb the property ladder. My only criticism is the complexity of the schemes and eligibility criteria. The intentions are noble, but the execution is poor.

The Help to Buy scheme

The Help to Buy (HTB) scheme helps first-time buyers purchase a newly built house or apartment. It's also available for one-off, self-build homes, but only applies to properties that cost €500,000 or less.

You can claim relief on the lesser of:
- €30,000
- 10% of the market value of a newly built property
- 10% of the approved valuation of a self-build property
- The income tax and DIRT you paid for the four years before the year you applied for the scheme. You cannot claim relief on PRSI or USC.

It is, in essence, a government-sponsored tax refund scheme to help first-time buyers pay a deposit on newly built homes.

At the time of publication, the maximum you can claim is €30,000. So, if your home is valued at €400,000, you still only claim the maximum €30,000 instead of the 10%. To qualify, there is also a loan-to-value ratio that must be met. The scheme has so far been extended to the end of 2024.

First Home Scheme

The First Home Scheme (FHS) is what's called a shared equity scheme. The government provides up to 30% of the property value for the same stake in your home. You can buy back the stake anytime, but this is not obligatory. By the sixth year, however, a service charge for the maintenance of the FHS will apply. This charge is a percentage of the amount the FHS paid when you bought the home and increases the longer you stay in the scheme. The charges range from 1.75% to 2.85%.

To be eligible, you must be a first-time buyer buying a new-build home. The scheme was extended to people building their own new homes, and every applicant must have the full deposit for the house.

It's also open to 'fresh start' applicants. They are people who previously owned a home but no longer have a financial interest in it because of divorce, separation or the end of a relationship. 'Fresh start' applicants can also be people who have gone through personal insolvency or bankruptcy.

The scheme is also available to people who want to buy their rental home because their landlord is selling the property. This version of the FHS is known as the Tenant Home Purchase Scheme and applies to second-hand homes.

It bridges the gap between the first-time buyer's deposit and the mortgage they can borrow. See the illustration below from the First Home Scheme website.

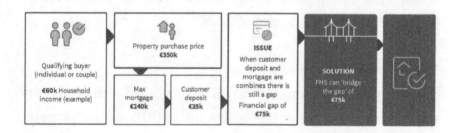

Local Authority Home Loan

The Local Authority Home Loan is a government-backed mortgage for first-time buyers and other limited applicants. They offer loans at a reduced interest rate to buy new and second-hand properties or to build a home. Local authorities provide loans at a 4% fixed-interest rate for up to twenty-five years (at the end of 2023).

The interest rates are fixed for the full term of the mortgage, so you have the same repayments for the loan's lifetime.

You can borrow 90% of the 'maximum market value', which depends on the property location. They increased in 2023 to €360,000 for houses in Dublin, Kildare and Wicklow, for example.

To qualify, you must be a first-time buyer or 'fresh start' applicant and be able to show evidence of 'insufficient offers of finance' from two banks. You must also have a gross salary of less than €70,000 for a single applicant and €85,000 for a couple. You must also have the full deposit and a good credit report. The scheme also has requirements for continuous employment or self-employment for two years.

Vacant Property Refurbishment Grant

The Vacant Property Refurbishment Grant provides funding so you can refurbish vacant and derelict homes. You may be eligible for the grant if you are refurbishing the vacant property to live there or rent the property out. You can get a grant of up to €50,000 to renovate a vacant property and up to €70,000 if the property is derelict.

Those who qualify for the Vacant Property Refurbishment Grant Scheme may also apply for home energy upgrade grants via the Sustainable Energy Authority of Ireland (SEAI). Grants are available under this scheme as high as €100,000.

One major criticism of the Vacant Property Refurbishment Grant Scheme is that you must complete the work before receiving the grant. This means you need the cash flow to complete the project first.

What is a lifetime loan mortgage?

A lifetime loan is a mortgage enabling a homeowner, typically over the age of sixty, to borrow against the value they have built up in their property. The owner gets a lump sum of cash at a fixed rate without the need to sell their house, trade down, move out, or make regular repayments. It's a form of equity release on your property.

Instead of making repayments on this mortgage, the finance company adds its interest to the loan balance, which grows over time. The loan is not repayable until after the borrower dies, permanently moves out, or the property is sold. With a lifetime loan, the borrower retains ownership of their home.

Currently, two types of lifetime loans are available – the standard and a green lifetime loan. The green lifetime loan is designed for people with an energy-efficient home or willing to invest in energy efficiency for their home. It comes with a reduced interest rate and is subject to certain qualifications.

Lifetime loans are not suitable for everyone, but they are a valuable financial tool for the over-sixties. So here are some other key points you need to know about them when considering whether they are a good fit for your needs.

- The interest rate is fixed for life, so you know exactly what will be repaid.
- You have the choice and ability to make optional repayments to help manage the loan balance.
- A 'no negative equity guarantee' is provided, which means you will never owe more than the value of your home.
-

Who is eligible for a lifetime loan?

Lifetime loans are available to people who are over sixty and who own their own home. The loan can only be secured against a permanent residence in Ireland worth at least €250,000 in Dublin or €175,000 elsewhere. The borrower must be the registered owner of the property. If there are two of you, the younger person must be 60 or older.

How much can be borrowed?

The maximum amount someone can borrow depends on their age when the loan is agreed, and the value of their property. The amount that can be borrowed starts at 15% of the property value at age 60 and rises 1% per year up to 40% for those aged eighty-five and older.

The minimum lifetime loan amount is €20,000, and the maximum is typically €500,000, but amounts above this are considered case by case.

A consultation with your financial planner will ensure the lifetime loan meets your financial needs.

Are there any restrictions on how I spend the lifetime loan?

No. Lifetime loans are designed to help meet your financial needs throughout retirement – whatever they may be – so borrowers are free to spend the money as they wish. The top reasons given by those over sixty who have applied for a lifetime loan are:

- Cash fund to maintain lifestyle or for a 'rainy day'
- Home improvements
- Cars and holidays
- To pay off existing mortgage or other debt
- Gifts to family and friends

What key benefits are there to a lifetime loan?

The primary benefit of lifetime loans is the ability to unlock the value of your home while retaining ownership and without having to move out. You receive a lump sum of money, which you don't have to repay, and you know you can stay in your home for life.

The fixed interest rate provides certainty about how the loan will grow. However, there is also flexibility – borrowers can reduce their loan balance by making repayments of up to 10% of their original loan amount each year without incurring a penalty.

The loan only becomes repayable if you sell your home, move from your home into long-term permanent care, or pass away.

The no negative equity guarantee means you never owe more than the value of your home. Neither you nor your estate will ever have to repay more than the net sale proceeds of the property, even if the loan balance exceeds this amount.

What about the small print?

The main thing to know is that if you choose not to make monthly repayments, interest is charged to the loan balance each month. The loan balance will increase over time with compound interest until it is repaid.

The future value of your equity in your home will reduce and may leave you and your estate with no equity remaining.

Are there alternatives to a lifetime loan?

A lifetime loan is only one option and may not be the right fit for everyone. Other alternatives for raising money or your standard of living during your pension years include:

- trading down
- sale of your house and renting accommodation
- letting part of your home
- applying for a standard mortgage
- support from family and friends
- existing savings and investments
- more efficient budgeting of income and expenditure

Who provides lifetime loans?

Spry Finance is the only lender in the Irish market currently offering lifetime loans to new customers. Launched in 2021, Spry Finance is 100% Irish-owned and headquartered in Dublin. It is part of a company, Seniors Money (Mortgages) Ireland DAC, which is regulated by the Central Bank of Ireland and has been operating in the Irish market since 2006.

At askpaul, we have an agency with Spry Finance, and we recommend that customers have a mortgage consultation with a financial planner to see if a lifetime loan is the right product to meet their personal financial needs and objectives.

What do the regulatory warnings mean?

You'll have heard the radio ads that end with an actor speed-reading regulatory warnings – or you'll see ads with small print concerning regulatory warnings. The Central Bank of Ireland demands these warnings be part of advertisements, but the lenders try to minimise them as much as possible.

We'll have a brief close-up of these warnings, as they're important.

- **Warning: If you do not keep up your repayments, you may lose your home.**
That's perfectly clear. But banks cannot take your house off you if you miss one payment. You are brought into a mortgage-arrears process.
- **Warning: If you do not meet the repayments on your loan, your account will go into arrears. This may affect your credit rating, which may limit your ability to access credit in the future.**
This applies to all loans and is reasonable and logical.
- **Warning: The cost of your monthly repayments may increase.**
This applies to anyone on a variable or tracker mortgage. It's pointing out that you are at the mercy of the macroeconomic environment. Fixed rates are impervious to any interest rate increases or decreases until the end of your term. Remember, when your fixed-rate term ends, the bank will bounce you into a variable rate.

- **Warning: You may have to pay charges if you pay off a fixed-rate loan early.**
  This isn't always applicable but is reasonable. With a fixed-rate mortgage, you sign a contract to lock into a rate for a specific period – so the lender will look for some compensation if you end the contract early.

What are the worst mortgages of all?

Any person whose mortgage has ended up in the hands of the so-called vulture funds, such as Mars Capital and Pepper, has my sympathies.

AIB, Bank of Ireland and other banks sold many non-performing loans to vulture funds especially since the 2008 financial crash. 'Non-performing loans' belong to many people who fell behind in payments because of losing their jobs, businesses or health since the global financial crash of 2008.

These funds do not offer their clients fixed rates and their interest rates are exorbitant – often between 7% and 10%. These people are 'mortgage prisoners' with no option to switch.

Vulture funds who buy these mortgages at huge discounts are not subject to the same regulatory standards as banks. The borrowers who end up in their clutches lose some protections they had with a regulated bank.

In an ongoing High Court case in November 2023, plaintiffs accused a vulture fund of charging them 8.5% interest. They claimed they're paying €7,400 more in interest a year than their original bank is charging customers.

Some vulture funds are accused of aggressive collection tactics, including pursuing repossessions to recoup their investment. Borrowers report being harangued by multiple daily phone calls. They are in constant fear of being pushed out of their homes.

Our state-owned banks delivered many people into the clutches of these largely opaque American enterprises. It will be interesting to watch the outcome of this High Court case, as it may have implications for thousands of other mortgage holders.

Why we need financial education – before getting a mortgage

When we get a car, we're taught how to drive it. Yet money is even more fundamental to our progress and security in life, and we are given no idea how to use it for our benefit. Financial education continues to be overlooked and is not getting the attention it needs.

Not equipping ourselves with the right educational tools to manage our finances is a terrible oversight. It's not our fault. It's our education system, the regulators and the Central Bank. Financial institutions and businesses can also play a huge part here. But this lack of financial education is never so apparent than when it comes to mortgages – the biggest financial outlays of our lives.

Two options might have saved a lot of financial heartache for people in this higher interest rate environment.

Switching

My company screamed from every rooftop to warn mortgage holders to switch to a fixed 2.5%–2.9% in 2022. We called clients and we put out the message via askpaul everywhere on social media. And we were busy switching mortgages, but nothing like we should have been.

I'm always astounded by some people's apathy. The people who listened and switched are saving thousands of euros yearly on their fixed rate – and that's thousands of euros after tax. Most others sleepwalked into losing thousands of their hard-earned money every year.

I can't explain this apathy. I assume it happens because people don't understand interest rates and their impact on repayments.

Maybe if people had the benefit of a sound financial education, they wouldn't be in the position where they're struggling with rising interest rates.

Because if you were one of those people who enjoyed a decade of 0% interest rates on a tracker mortgage, you would have known what to do. If you had basic financial literacy, you would have seen the writing on the wall about rising interest rates and switched to a fixed rate.

There are still opportunities for people to switch now, albeit at higher rates. Tracker mortgage holders may switch to lower fixed-rate options, but take advice before you do.

Saving

Some of you now have monthly mortgage repayments that are €500 higher than two years ago. Yet you can find that €500 because you don't want to default on a mortgage repayment. Everyone adapts and changes their spending habits to cope with these unexpected increases.

What if you had saved €500 monthly for ten years? Instead of simply enjoying the benefits of a low-cost mortgage for years, you could have redeployed those savings into more productive uses.

Without even investing it, you would have €60,000 today. You could have used that surplus cash to overpay your mortgage so that it would be much reduced by now or you would have a nice nest egg to weather any of these financial hits. What do you have to show for that €500 extra money today?

The problem is that most people were blindly unaware that this gravy train of 1% and low-interest rate mortgages would not last for ever. They had little awareness of how an uptick in interest rates could affect them. This is an example of how poor financial education affects many people.

CLIENT CASE
SEAN & CIARA, AGED 33

The table on p271 shows a mortgage repayment schedule for Sean and Ciara who want to borrow €380,000 over twenty-five years fixed at 4.5%. The focus here is not the monthly repayments of €2,112.16 but the interest costs over twenty-five years.

Sean and Ciara's mortgage interest rates if paid normally

If Sean and Ciara take a loan of €380,000, they'll repay €633,649 over the mortgage term – this is why banks are so profitable. The cost of interest over twenty-five years is €253,649.

Full monthly repayments €2,112.16 Initial interest only €1,425.00 Total interest charged €253,649.02

Total cost of mortgage €633,649.02

YEAR	PAYMENT DATE	BEGINNING BALANCE (€)	SCHEDULED PAYMENT (€)	EXTRA PAYMENT (€)	TOTAL PAYMENT (€)	CAPITAL (€)	INTEREST (€)	BALANCE (€)
1	01-11-24	380,000.00	25,345.96	00.00	25,345.96	8,418.18	16,927.78	371,581.82
2	01-11-25	371,581.82	25,345.96	00.00	25,345.96	8,804.91	16,541.05	362,776.91
3	01-11-26	362,776.91	25,345.96	00.00	25,345.96	9,209.40	16,136.56	353,567.51
4	01-11-27	353,567.51	25,345.96	00.00	25,345.96	9,632.48	15,713.48	343,935.03
5	01-11-28	343,935.03	25,345.96	00.00	25,345.96	10,075.00	15,270.96	333,860.03
6	01-11-29	333,860.03	25,345.96	00.00	25,345.96	10,537.84	14,808.12	323,322.19
7	01-11-30	323,322.19	25,345.96	00.00	25,345.96	11,021.95	14,324.01	312,300.25
8	01-11-31	312,300.25	25,345.96	00.00	25,345.96	11,528.29	13,817.67	300,771.95
9	01-11-32	300,771.95	25,345.96	00.00	25,345.96	12,057.90	13,288.06	288,714.05
10	01-11-33	288,714.05	25,345.96	00.00	25,345.96	12,611.84	12,734.12	276,102.22
11	01-11-34	276,102.22	25,345.96	00.00	25,345.96	13,191.22	12,154.74	262,910.99
12	01-11-35	262,910.99	25,345.96	00.00	25,345.96	13,797.23	11,548.73	249,113.76
13	01-11-36	249,113.76	25,345.96	00.00	25,345.96	14,431.07	10,914.89	234,682.70
14	01-11-37	234,668.70	25,345.96	00.00	25,345.96	15,094.03	10,251.93	219,588.67
15	01-11-38	219,588.67	25,345.96	00.00	25,345.96	15,787.45	9,558.51	203,801.22
16	01-11-39	203,801.22	25,345.96	00.00	25,345.96	16,512.72	8,833.24	187,288.50
17	01-11-40	187,288.50	25,345.96	00.00	25,345.96	17,271.31	8,074.65	170,017.19
18	01-11-41	170,017.19	25,345.96	00.00	25,345.96	18,064.75	7,281.21	151,952.44
19	01-11-42	151,952.44	25,345.96	00.00	25,345.96	18,894.64	6,451.32	133,057.80
20	01-11-43	133,057.80	25,345.96	00.00	25,345.96	19,762.66	5,583.30	113,295.14
21	01-11-44	113,295.14	25,345.96	00.00	25,345.96	20,670.55	4,675.41	92,624.58
22	01-11-45	92,624.58	25,345.96	00.00	25,345.96	21,620.15	3,725.81	71,004.43
23	01-11-46	71,004.43	25,345.96	00.00	25,345.96	22,613.38	2,732.58	48,391.05
24	01-11-47	48,391.05	25,345.96	00.00	25,345.96	23,652.24	1,693.73	24,738.81
25	01-11-48	24,738.81	25,345.96	00.00	25,345.96	24,738.81	607.15	000.00

Note: Year 1 – the total payment is €25,345.96 or €2,112.16 monthly. However, the capital reduces by only €8,418.18, meaning the interest to the bank is €16,927 (double the capital reduction).

Note: Year 11 – it is not until then that Sean and Ciara will see the reduction in the capital amount is more than the interest payments to the bank.

Note: Year 25 – the interest payment is only €607.15, and the capital paid is €24,738.

What does this mean? It means the bank looks after itself first. The bank takes most of the repayment as interest first and only reduces Sean and Ciara's loan later. Much later.

The lesson here is if you have a mortgage or are considering a mortgage, make sure you look after *yourself* first. Understand how mortgages work. Know how to play the system.

Sean and Ciara's mortgage interest rates with overpayment

The table on p273 is an example of how Sean and Ciara can look after themselves.

The mortgage terms are the same: €380,000 over twenty-five years fixed at 4.5%. This time, the borrowers overpay €100 per week or €400 per month.

Full monthly repayments €2,512.36 Initial interest only €1,425.00 Total interest charged €182,150.54 Total cost of mortgage €562,150.54 Term reduced by 76 months Amount saved €71,498.48

YEAR	PAYMENT DATE	BEGINNING BALANCE (€)	SCHEDULED PAYMENT (€)	EXTRA PAYMENT (€)	TOTAL PAYMENT (€)	CAPITAL (€)	INTEREST (€)	BALANCE (€)
1	01-11-24	380,000.00	25,345.96	4,800.00	30,145.96	13,318.43	16,827.54	366,681.57
2	01-11-25	366,681.57	25,345.96	4,800.00	30,145.96	13,930.27	16,251.69	352,751.30
3	01-11-26	352,751.30	25,345.96	4,800.00	30,145.96	14,570.23	15,575.73	338,181.08
4	01-11-27	338,181.08	25,345.96	4,800.00	30,145.96	15,239.58	14,906.38	332,941.50
5	01-11-28	322,941.50	25,345.96	4,800.00	30,145.96	15,939.68	14,206.28	307,001.81
6	01-11-29	307,001.81	25,345.96	4,800.00	30,145.96	16,671.95	13,474.01	290,329.86
7	01-11-30	290,329.86	25,345.96	4,800.00	30,145.96	17,437.86	12,708.10	272,892.01
8	01-11-31	272,892.01	25,345.96	4,800.00	30,145.96	18,238.95	11,907.01	254,653.06
9	01-11-32	254,653.06	25,345.96	4,800.00	30,145.96	19,076.84	11,069.12	235,576.22
10	01-11-33	235,576.22	25,345.96	4,800.00	30,145.96	19,953.23	10,192.73	215,622.99
11	01-11-34	215,622.99	25,345.96	4,800.00	30,145.96	20,869.88	9,276.08	194,753.11
12	01-11-35	194,753.11	25,345.96	4,800.00	30,145.96	21,828.64	8,317.33	172,924.47
13	01-11-36	172,924.47	25,345.96	4,800.00	30,145.96	22,831.44	7,314.52	150,093.03
14	01-11-37	150,093.03	25,345.96	4,800.00	30,145.96	23,880.31	6,265.65	126,212.72
15	01-11-38	126,212.72	25,345.96	4,800.00	30,145.96	24,977.37	5,168.59	101,235.35
16	01-11-39	101,235.35	25,345.96	4,800.00	30,145.96	26,124.83	4,021.14	75,110.53
17	01-11-40	75,110.53	25,345.96	4,800.00	30,145.96	27,324.99	2,820.97	47,785.53
18	01-11-41	47,785.53	25,345.96	4,800.00	30,145.96	28,580.30	1,565.66	19,205.23
19	01-11-42	19,205.23	25,345.96	2,800.00	19,523.24	19,205.23	318.01	000.00

> The first thing to note here is the reduction in the cost of interest from €253,649 to €182,150. This means a reduction in interest payments of €71,499.
>
> Note: Year 19 – the mortgage ends six years early. Sean and Ciara can also have a nineteen-year mortgage instead of paying for twenty-five years.

Where is the mortgage market going in 2024?

I estimate that ECB interest rates will remain high in 2024 as high inflation rates continue. If inflation falls substantially in 2024 (which is unlikely), you may see one or two rate drops in the ECB rate.

However, whatever happens with the ECB, I expect Irish banks to increase their fixed rates across the board in 2024 and 2025. The problem is that the banks have a lot of room for movement in the fixed and variable rates they currently offer customers. So far, they have relied on free, or almost free, money from Irish depositors to fund their mortgages. However, if the banks follow the ECB's rate increases, the best five-year fixed rate could be around 5.75%.

So, I still recommend long-term fixing in early 2024.

Whatever happens, the bad news is we're unlikely to see a return to the rock-bottom rates that we enjoyed for many years until 2022.

That means we may be sleepwalking into a new mortgage crisis. Many borrowers whose fixed rates of 2.5% are ending will re-enter a market where their rates may double. Anyone nearing the end of a fixed-term rate should seek advice now.

I also recommend that if you can overpay your mortgage, you should.

If rising mortgage interest rates leave you struggling, there are options. Look into debt restructuring and engage a personal insolvency practitioner (PIP). We discussed this option in more detail in Section 2 (Managing Your Debt).

Where does a mortgage fit with a financial plan?

If you plan to live into retirement, the last thing you want to be is a renter. Even though a home is an illiquid and inflexible asset, it gives us security and stability, especially in retirement. Buying our own house should be an aspiration for most of us. You don't want the pressure of funding a roof over your head in retirement, especially if you rely on the state pension or only have a small private pension.

Instead of paying rent to a landlord, your mortgage payments build equity in your home over time. A mortgage is like a forced savings plan that grows as your home increases in value. Every payment you make towards your mortgage is money invested in your own wealth, rather than a landlord's.

The target should be to clear the mortgage by retirement. That's because paying rent or a mortgage will be unfeasible for many of us when we retire. We know only six in ten Irish workers have a private pension and many of those are funding it inadequately.

By owning your property, you could also boost your pension. The rent-a-room relief scheme, for example, lets you earn up to €14,000 per year tax-free.

And you have the option to downsize your property and move to a smaller home with a nice cash nest egg for your pension.

As discussed above, the over-sixties can also boost their pensions by getting a lifetime loan on their home. This form of equity release is a cash loan on the value of your house and may be a solution if you need cash but want to stay in your home.

Whether you're single, a couple, renting or living at home, the quicker you get a mortgage, the easier it will be to protect your financial future. Keeping a roof over your head is your biggest financial outlay. Pay it sooner rather than later and make a plan to own your own home.

Your 7-point action plan to get mortgage fit

- **Check your credit score.** Get a copy of your credit report from the Central Credit Register. (Details above.) A good credit score is crucial for a favourable mortgage rate. If your score needs improvement, address any outstanding issues and pay off debts.
- **Clear your debts.** Outstanding loans, credit-card debt, car finance and overdrafts will affect the amount a bank is willing to lend to you. At the very least, minimise your debts and ensure all payments are up to date.
- **Assess your finances and reduce your outgoings.** Lenders want mortgage and insurance costs not to exceed 35% of your net income

(earnings after tax, PRSI, etc.). TThe lenders must see a healthy 'cushion' of cash in your account at the end of every month.

Start saving. Demonstrate a regular savings history, as it's evidence of your ability to manage regular payments. Also, the bigger your deposit, the smaller the mortgage you'll need. First-time buyers will need a minimum deposit of 10% under the current Central Bank rules.

- **Establish a steady employment record.** Lenders prefer borrowers who have a stable employment history. Don't change jobs when you're about to buy a house. A new job might be worth delaying until after you secure your mortgage.

- **Get your documents in order.** Lenders require certain proofs before considering your application: proof of identification, address and income, and bank statements for at least the previous six months. Make sure nothing in those bank statements worries them – like money coming in or out of betting apps.

- **Plan for additional costs in the buying process.** Whatever you think you'll need, double it. Stamp duty, solicitor's fees, valuation fees and other administrative costs could add to your initial outlay. Be sure to factor these into your budget to avoid any unpleasant surprises.

SECTION 7
PENSIONS

Let's begin our journey into pensions with a quick quiz:

- Do you want to live for twenty or thirty years after you stop working?
- Would you like to be financially comfortable during this period?

Okay, that isn't much of a quiz. I've never met a client who didn't answer yes to both these questions. However, there's no magic wand when it comes to pensions. The ability to live in comfort after you stop earning does not happen automatically. That's why we need to make a financial plan for our retirement.

A pensions crisis in Ireland is fast approaching. (I will discuss this below.) My hope is that this section may help you avert a crisis in your own pension pot. If you are in your twenties, feeling bulletproof and forever young, this book is not here to convince you to start thinking about a pension. When you think of pensions, someone who's sixty-five, grey and old may come to mind. It only seems like five minutes ago when I was in my twenties, but now I'm grey and middle-aged. Trust me, it comes around fairly quickly.

If you can invest in a pension in your twenties, do it. But I understand you may have other priorities, like getting on the property ladder.

Everyone else, please read on and take the first proactive step to bolster your pension and protect the future *you*. You're the only one who can take care of your affairs, so it's up to you to take control of your financial destiny.

What is a pension?

Imagine a pension as a special treasure chest for your future. Every time you earn some income during your working life, you lock a bit into the pension treasure chest. While your money lies in the treasure chest, magic elves top it up with extra money. Then, one day, you get older and stop working and open that treasure chest full of gold. And you live happily ever after. That's the fairy-tale ending, anyway.

A pension is a form of long-term savings and investment that helps secure financial stability in your old age when you are no longer working. If it's managed well, a pension is like a savings and investment plan on steroids.

There are state pensions and personal pensions. All workers contribute to the Irish state pension during their working lives through compulsory social-insurance payments known as PRSI contributions.

Many people supplement the state pension by contributing to a personal pension or company pension plan. This money is invested in funds by authorised pension providers, often life-assurance companies. We discuss these funds in more detail in Section 3 (Saving and Investing).

The only difference between a normal investment fund and a personal or company pension is that you can't typically access your pension until you are sixty. If you have an old company pension plan from a previous employment you may be able to access this pension from fifty. This pension fund then provides a regular income stream payment for the rest of your life or a money pot in which you drawn down at your discretion. It's important to note that you may outlive your pension pot if it's not managed correctly before and after retirement. This is why having an active financial plan in place is so important when it comes to retirement planning.

Why do we have pensions?

Nobody likes to think of growing old, but there comes a day in most people's lives when they stop working. For some, they want to stop working at retirement age, typically sixty-five. Many people, especially those with well-funded pensions, look forward to retiring. They see it as a new chapter of life where they can enjoy their hobbies, take up new pursuits or travel. Other people have to stop work because of illness and some employers force workers to stop working at sixty-five.

Pensions are designed to replace our earnings and provide a steady income stream when we no longer earn a regular salary. They ensure we can maintain a certain standard of living, cover essential expenses and live without financial stress. Overall, pensions provide income security and stability in retirement and are crucial in preventing poverty among the older population.

Who should have a pension?

Everyone who wants to avoid poverty and dependence in old age should contribute to a pension. In 2024, if you're aged sixty-six or over and are lucky enough to qualify for the full state pension, you will receive €277.30 per week. (And it's important to emphasise that not everyone is entitled to that full payment. See below for more details.) This is not a substantial amount of money and only provides us with a basic standard of living.

The financial sustainability of the state pension and its ability to support a growing number of retired people is also a growing concern. The government has been tweaking and raising the eligibility criteria for a state pension. Who knows what the requirements demanded for a pension will be in ten or twenty years?

Rather than relying solely on a state pension, we must plan and save for our own retirement. The good news is that the government offers generous tax incentives to encourage personal pension savings, but more of that below.

How many people have pensions?

Pensions, pensions, pensions … where did it all go wrong? Unfortunately, not enough people are investing in a pension, and those who do are not investing enough.

I have to admit, the finance industry has a lot to do with it. The industry has failed you. The industry has failed on messaging, has failed on marketing, and fails to win hearts and minds despite the fantastic financial incentives to start personal pensions.

For a start, the language used in the pensions industry is impenetrable. Pensions are filled with jargon and acronyms like PRB, PRSAs, ARFs, AVCs and PPPs. We'll be discussing a few of these relevant acronyms later, even though I can almost see your eyes glazing over as I write this. It's little wonder that people find it hard to get motivated about pensions.

Ireland's Central Statistics Office conducted a *Pension Coverage Survey* in 2022 and reported:

- Only six in ten people in the Irish workforce have some sort of private pension.
- Nearly six in ten workers with *no* pension coverage stated that the state pension was the expected primary source of income for them on retirement.
- More than one-quarter (26%) with *no* pension coverage had not yet decided what their main source of income would be.

This is really concerning because, as it stands, the state pension provides a very basic standard of living. It may just about pay the electricity bill and feed a person, but it will not provide a comfortable retirement.

It's also concerning that many people are unaware that their private pensions are underfunded. The average pension pot in Ireland is €100,000 to €130,000. That might seem like a sizeable sum, but not when you consider this income needs to last for twenty to twenty-five years – or more. Our life expectancy is increasing because of medical improvements and healthier lifestyles.

To make matters worse, this is an expensive country. In figures published in 2023, the European Commission revealed household expenditure on goods and services in Ireland cost 46% above the EU average. Only Switzerland and Iceland had higher consumer prices than this country. We are facing retirement in one of the most expensive countries in Europe.

Do the figures. Will you be able to live comfortably when you stop working?

What is the pension time bomb?

I don't like being negative, but the news gets worse. We are facing a pension time bomb that is about to explode.

By the time many of us reach retirement age, I doubt that the Irish state pension will exist in its current form. I've even heard it referred to as a Ponzi scheme, which is hard to hear. However, there may be some truth to this. The government advises us to fund our pensions, but they have failed to do that themselves. No single pot of money or fund is devoted exclusively to state pensions. We do not have a sovereign wealth fund like Norway, built after their substantial oil discoveries in the 1960s.

Social-welfare benefits and the current state pension are paid out of current tax receipts received each year. So, pensioners are funded from PRSI, USC, income tax, VAT and corporation tax.

The former minister for finance, Charlie McCreevy, did attempt to set aside surplus taxes for the National Pension Reserve Fund (NPRF) and, by 2008, it had accumulated €25 billion to fund our future pension needs. It might have grown to €100 billion by now if it had been left untouched. However, the fund was raided to bail out the Irish banks following the global financial crisis that started in 2008. (See 'What was the global financial crash of 2008?' Section 1 (Personal Budgeting).)

Currently, the country only has €6 billion in a fund invested in low-risk government bonds. It's a drop in the ocean compared to the money needed to fund future state-pension liabilities.

Of course, we could have used funds from the Irish corporate tax boom to set up such a pension pot. The country has enjoyed unprecedented tax windfalls from corporate taxes. These come from a few large US tech and pharma companies who have their European headquarters in Ireland. Corporate taxes have rocketed, hitting record highs, with €22.6 billion coming into Ireland's national coffers in 2022.

The government is discussing establishing a sovereign wealth fund next year to channel some of our bumper budget surpluses into future pensions. Of course, it's easy to talk about it. So far, there's been little political appetite in Ireland for thinking decades ahead. Through our taxes, we're paying into something with a vague promise of returns at a later date. Will there be enough money to fund our pensions in twenty years? Unless something drastically changes, it's unlikely there will be.

The big problem with pensions is our demographics. Ireland's population is ageing because of increased life expectancy and falling birth rates. As a result, our working-age population is declining, and the proportion of older adults relying on state pensions is increasing. A smaller working population is unlikely to meet the financial demands of a larger retired population.

Pensions are not a problem now because Ireland has five workers paying taxes to fund every person receiving the state pension. But, by the year 2050, this ratio will dramatically reduce to two workers paying taxes for every one retiree.

Demographics are destiny. If you are under fifty, you must be more proactive than those who will retire in five years.

The government is already scrambling to reform the pension system to address this pension time bomb. The state pension age was to rise to sixty-seven in 2021, but the move was unpopular and so the government reversed the change.

There have been other changes over the years. Those who reached pension age before 2002 only needed 156 paid contributions (three years' contributions) to qualify for a contributory state pension. Under the current system, you need at least 520 paid contributions to be eligible for a pension (ten years' contributions).

The government is also making other tweaks to keep people working for longer. From January 2024, you can defer collecting your pension to anytime between the ages of sixty-six and seventy. This can increase your contributions to meet the minimum qualifying condition of 520 (ten years) for state pension (contributory) or help reach the current maximum of 2,080 (forty years).

However, it's only a matter of time before the strain on our social-welfare system becomes too much. The worry is that the entitlement to a contributory state pension will change. The eligibility criteria for the state pension are expected to be continually under review. In the future, the state pension may be means-tested, reduced or even removed for specific sections of the population.

The big question is how long will the state be able to maintain adequate levels of support for retirees? In the past, at least many retirees owned their own homes. However, a growing number of future retirees will never own a home. How will they meet the costs of renting accommodation in their retirement?

Where will state pensions be in twenty years' time? Things will be different, that's for sure. We are moving to an age of individualisation, which means *you look after you*. The age of guaranteed pensions from jobs is gone. We have moved to an era of *what you put in is what you'll get out*.

Yet, many people are not getting the message that they cannot rely on the state pension. It provides barely enough to survive on right now, and the future of the state pension and eligibility is uncertain. It's going to become more and more essential that you provide for your own retirement.

Why is the pensions time bomb worse for women?

Thankfully, we're all living longer. However, women, on average, live five years more than men. As a result, they need to be funded for longer in retirement.

But, women in the EU earn 13% less per hour than men. This disgraceful and startling statistic has negative connotations for women trying to fund their pension. This gender pay gap is handicapping them as they plan for their retirement.

Women also tend to take more time off work (extended

maternity leave, parental leave, etc.) to look after children. Often, they are the ones who take time off to care for sick relatives. Unpaid time away from the workforce can also mean a reduction in pension contributions.

For this reason and others, women are estimated to retire with a pension fund that is 22% less than equivalent male workers. Then, they also have the challenge of making this smaller pension last longer. Unfortunately, it will take years, if not decades, to remedy these forms of gender discrimination.

I give particular advice to clients who are planning a family and are in a company or civil-service pension scheme. I always recommend that they consider making additional voluntary contributions (AVCs – we'll be discussing these later) into their pension before they take unpaid leave or in the year after they return to work.

If you're a female reader, you must be aware of the extra pension hurdles you face and ensure you aren't left behind.

What are the different pensions?

The state pension (contributory)
The government provides most Irish citizens with a state pension to support them in their retirement.

Anyone over sixty-six with enough pay-related social insurance (PRSI) contributions may receive the state pension. The amount you get depends on how many years you contribute to the Irish social-insurance system and how many contributions you make each year.

The Department of Social Protection manages the state pension scheme in Ireland. Their contributions system is complicated, and the exact number of contributions required varies. When you have 520 'Reckonable Contributions' (ten years), you will qualify for a state pension – though not necessarily the full pension.

If you're unsure how many years you have paid PRSI or worried about qualifying, you can check your records by visiting https://services.mywelfare.ie. You will need your MyGovID login details to check your records.

As I've said, in 2024 the maximum state pension in Ireland for a person aged sixty-six or over is €277.30 per week. State pensions provide a basic income level to support individuals and help prevent poverty among retirees. However, an annual income of around €14,000 (if you qualify for the full pension) means you won't exactly live happily ever after.

The state pension (non-contributory)

The non-contributory state pension is for people aged sixty-six and over who do not qualify for a state pension (contributory). Unlike the contributory pension, this is a 'means-tested' payment. This means your income must be below a certain level for you to qualify. In a means test, the Department of Social Protection examines all your sources of income and that of your spouse, civil partner or cohabitant. The maximum personal rate you will receive for the non-contributory pension is €254. This can increase if you have an adult dependent or a child dependent. The payment also increases to €264 when you reach eighty years of age.

The occupational pension

Employers often offer an occupational pension as an additional benefit to their employees. The occupational or company pension is a retirement savings plan specific to that workplace. Employees usually contribute a portion of their salary to the pension scheme and the employer may also contribute on their behalf.

The accumulated funds in the occupational pension scheme are invested to grow over time. When the individual retires, they receive a regular income from the pension fund they've built up.

The problem is that many workers with an occupational pension sit back and think they're sorted. Then, they're shocked when they realise how small their fund is as they get close to retirement. Remember, it's your responsibility to look after your pension planning, not your employer's.

The personal pension

A personal pension is a pension plan you arrange independently rather than through your employer. It is a private savings plan designed to help you save for retirement. Many people who are self-employed or those who do not have access to an occupational pension scheme take out personal pensions.

You can make monthly payments or an annual lump-sum contribution into a personal pension. A life assurance or investment company invests these contributions in funds or assets. By contributing regularly to a pension over your working years, you can accumulate a significant sum of money to support you during retirement. By starting early enough, you can really amass a good pension pot.

You can use the personal pension fund to receive a regular income and a lump sum upon retirement. Having a private pension will also supplement any state benefits or other sources of income you may have.

If you have neither a company nor a personal pension, I'd urge you to consider talking to a financial planner. This doesn't mean you need to start contributing today. It means you have the discussion, assess your options and put a pension in your plan at some point.

The public-service pension

Public-service pensions offer far more generous benefits and security than the state pension. Public-service pensions are occupational pension schemes set up by the government for employees in the public service, local authorities or semi-state companies. They are paid to public-service employees, such as civil servants, teachers, nurses and members of the defence forces.

Semi-state pensions are paid to workers in government-owned or part-owned entities in sectors like energy, transport or telecommunications.

The public-service pension is exceptionally generous from an investment and actuarial perspective. And, unfortunately, the government has no secret investment strategy that enables them to pay such high pensions to workers in this sector.

The public-sector pension is paid from the same taxes that fund the state pension, social welfare, etc. I don't begrudge anyone receiving an excellent public-service pension – like many, I have immediate family, close relatives and friends working in the civil service. At a macro level, however, I have concerns about the sustainability of paying these pensions. Because when it comes to public-service and private-sector pensions, we're not comparing apples with apples. If the private sector is apples, the public-sector pension is more like luxurious avocados.

Most public-sector pensions are defined-benefit schemes. This means that their pensions are based on pay at retirement (for pre-2013 entrants). However, the rules have been tightened over the past decade. The pensions for those who joined the public service after 2013 are based on an average of pay and the number of years in the scheme.

The truth is public-sector pension schemes in Ireland can be very confusing. Many public-sector employees are unclear what their pension will be. Some can bolster their pensions by making additional voluntary contributions (AVCs). Everyone in the public service should seek advice on planning for their retirement and making the best use of AVCs.

CLIENT CASE

PAT, AGED 35

Pat is a public-sector worker who came to us last year. He had several AVCs simply because he was sold them. He didn't understand the fees or charges associated with his AVCs or the investment strategy behind them.

A financial planner convinced him of the benefits of an AVC with a spreadsheet of the predicted growth over thirty years. This is a classic case of the 'spreadsheet planner' at work.

There's no doubt that AVCs can be beneficial for both public- and private-sector workers. However, please be cautious about who you buy from. Many in the finance sector are heavily remunerated by AVC sales, which can compromise their impartiality.

Everything on the spreadsheet looked great, but it didn't know my client's age, financial goals or where he was in life. It didn't know that my client already had an amazing public-service pension. The 'planner' did but chose to ignore it.

What is the auto-enrolment pension scheme in Ireland?

Some of you may know about auto-enrolment, but many won't. Unfortunately, an auto-enrolment scheme remains on the distant horizon for Irish workers.

Auto-enrolment pension schemes ensure people save for retirement with little effort or thinking about it. The scheme is like a savings account you automatically contribute to from your monthly salary. Your employer automatically signs you up for a pension scheme so that a portion of your monthly salary will go towards your pension.

The problems of an ageing population are not unique to

Ireland. Many Western countries know that their state pensions are unsustainable and must find a new way to avert poverty in retirement. New Zealand, Australia and the UK have already introduced automatic pension-saving schemes for workers to help combat pension poverty.

The Irish government has been talking about introducing the same regime to help automate pension savings. However, that's all it has done. They launched a commission into this as far back as 2007, but sixteen years later, we still don't have auto-enrolment. The start date for the government's auto-enrolment scheme has been pushed out to the second half of 2024. However, even that target date for starting the project is slipping.

If it ever goes ahead, the plans for auto-enrolment are to see everyone earning more than €20,000 a year and aged between twenty-three and sixty enrolled in a private-pension scheme. Workers will be signed up to a pension scheme by default, though they can opt out.

It's a terrible shame and a wasted opportunity that this has not happened. We have a pension crisis hurtling towards us, and people are still not saving enough for their retirement. It's clear we can't rely on the government to do the right thing.

That's why we need to take personal responsibility and take control of our own financial affairs. Please don't wait for the government to introduce auto-enrolment. Talk to someone about starting a pension if you are not already in one.

What are the tax advantages if I contribute to a private pension?

Imagine if someone said, 'Give me €60, and I can instantly turn it into €100.' Imagine if the same person also offered to turn €600 into €1,000 or €6,000 into €10,000. You would undoubtedly say, 'Yes, please!'

An instantaneous 66% return on your money is an excellent investment. And that, folks, is the cornerstone of the Irish government's tax incentives to help you save for your pension. Any money you put into your pension fund has tax advantages.

Take someone called Mary. As Mary starts working and becomes a taxpayer, she can receive tax relief on her pension contributions. For every euro she contributes to her pension, the government will also contribute a portion of the tax she has paid on her earnings.

If Mary is on the higher rate of tax, she is eligible for a higher rate of tax relief on her private pension contributions. In Ireland, the higher rate of tax relief is 40%.

So, if Mary contributes €100 to her private pension, the cost after tax relief is:

€100 – (€100 x 40%)

= €100 – €40

= €60

Therefore, it only costs Mary €60 after the higher rate of tax relief of 40% is applied to make a €100 contribution to her private pension. Similarly, it will cost her €6,000 to make a

€10,000 contribution to her retirement. Over many years, she may save €100,000 in her pension, but it will have only cost her €60,000.

If Mary is a standard-rate taxpayer, she will receive tax relief at the standard rate, which is currently 20%. As a result, if she contributes €100 to her private pension, it will only cost her €80 after the tax relief is applied. It seems incredible to me that so many in the private-sector workforce are missing out on these fantastic tax benefits.

The other advantage of pensions is that they grow tax free for decades. The Revenue Commissioners do not tax pension growth. This benefit should not be overlooked, as tax-free compound interest is like adding financial steroids to your pension.

What happens when you go from a salary to the state pension?

Everything is rosy when you earn a good monthly salary. When you watch your expenses and spend less than you earn, nothing should go wildly wrong.

However, suddenly retirement looms. Let's return to Mary, who has a good salary of €80,000 or €4,300 after tax each month until she retires at age sixty-six. For some reason, Mary decided against taking advantage of the tax incentives and did not fund a personal pension. She will rely on the state pension, so, overnight, her income drops to €277.30 a week. What does that look like?

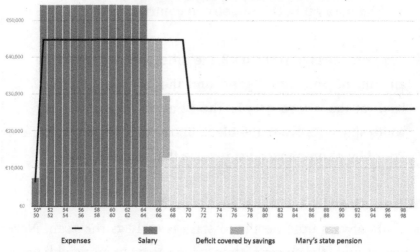

CASH FLOW FORECAST (ASKPAUL EXAMPLE)

Expenses   Salary   Deficit covered by savings   Mary's state pension

- The black line is Mary's everyday expenses.
- The black line dipping is Mary clearing her mortgage at last.
- The darkest grey bars are Mary's income.
- The lightest grey colour is the state pension.
- The white gap between the black line and the light-grey bars is Mary's problem. Overnight, she has to cut her monthly spending until the black line lowers to the light-grey bars.

Quiz

What is the pension gap?

1. The time between retirement and the start of receiving pension payments.
2. The difference between the pension amount needed and the amount received.
3. The space where pensions are typically held for safekeeping.

> 4.   The interval between pension contributions.
>
> Yes, you guessed right. It's 2, the difference between the amount of pension needed and the amount received. Look at the above graph. The pension gap is the big white space between the black line and light-grey bars. Poor Mary somehow must resolve that pension gap.

When should I start a pension?

I would always urge people to start as early as they can. Never underestimate the power of time to increase your money. However, there's no point in setting up a pension to the detriment of other impending financial needs.

Why would you start a pension if you have high-interest credit-card debt? Or you're still living at home with your parents. Here, your priorities are to get your finances in order and get on the property ladder.

Of course, for a multitude of reasons, you may come to pension planning later in life:

- You didn't have the earning power to contribute to a pension.
- Your priority was a mortgage, a new business, children, crèche fees, etc.
- You planned to get a pension but never got around to it. (More common than you think.)

No need to fret. Starting late is okay too. If you are lucky enough to be able to start in your forties or fifties, you can still take action and remedy this.

Personal Retirement Savings Accounts

Self-employed people can provide for their retirement using personal pensions or Personal Retirement Savings Accounts (PRSAs).

Revenue provides generous tax reliefs for self-employed people looking to provide for their retirement. These reliefs also apply to occupational pension schemes. You can save up to 40% of your net relevant earnings (up to a salary cap of €115,000). You can also get tax relief on your contribution at the marginal tax rate.

However, the threshold for tax relief is age related and subject to the salary cap as follows.

Some of you will find you're only positioned to start a pension in your early fifties. You may have paid your mortgage or raised the kids and have more disposable income.

As the table below illustrates, you can start super-charging your retirement with a regular pension contribution of up to 30% of your net earnings. The tax regime in Ireland recognises a need to support those who start funding a pension later in life.

AGE IN TAX YEAR	PERSONAL CONTRIBUTION
Under 30	15% net relevant earnings
30–39	20% net relevant earnings
40–49	25% net relevant earnings
50–54	30% net relevant earnings
55–59	35% net relevant earnings
60 and over	40% net relevant earnings

How to turn €50,000 into €300,000

Say you invest €250 per month over thirty years into a pension.

Tax relief of 40% means it only costs you €150 a month. (Tax relief at 20% reduces the cost to €200 a month.)

Thirty years later, after paying as little as €150 a month, you will have a fund of €304,999. This is assuming an 8% per annum average return and a 1% management charge or a net increase of 7% per annum. You have transformed €54,000 of payments into more than €300,000.

What are the forgotten pensions?

Once upon a time, people got jobs in the bank or the ESB and were delighted to have relatively secure, pensionable employment. Pre-2000, it wasn't unusual to have the same position for thirty-plus years. You did your time, and the company took care of you afterwards with their pension scheme.

However, the corporate world and worker behaviour have changed dramatically in recent decades. The era of the job-for-life is over, and many people go through several career changes during their working life. Employees today are temporary, contract, freelance or part-time. Many workers have never had permanent jobs. Instead, they have 'fixed-term contracts', and companies let them go when the contract ends. Many younger workers are not interested in 'staying put'.

Some employers try to entice workers to stay with benefits, such as pension schemes. However, job mobility continues, meaning some workers end up with four or more pensions left behind with different companies.

They often forget these pensions in the upheaval of leaving a company and starting a new job. Yes, they mean to sort out the pension, but then a decade passes and they move roles again, compounding another pension problem.

When you leave a job, there are a few options regarding what can happen to that pension. They can vary depending on the employer's policies and the pension scheme.

- Leave it with the old employer: This is not generally advisable, but you can often leave your occupational pension with your previous employer. You won't be able to make any further contributions to the pension. Still, your accumulated funds should remain invested and continue growing until retirement age.
- Transfer it to a new employer's scheme: If your new employer offers an occupational pension scheme, you can often transfer your previous occupational pension into the new one. This enables you to consolidate your pension savings into one account, making it easier to manage your retirement funds.
- Transfer it to a personal pension: Instead of transferring your pension to a new employer's scheme, you can move it into a personal-pension arrangement. By doing this, you gain more control over your pension savings. You can select your own investment options to suit your retirement goals and risk preferences.

The disadvantages of leaving a pension with an old employer include:

- Former employers' pension schemes are not obligated to provide you with updates on how your pension is managed or invested.

- You may be in the dark about their investment decisions.
- You also will not know the associated charges or increases in costs within the fund or if it is outperforming inflation.
- Not looking after your pensions can affect your retirement goals.

If you have pension pots with previous employers, get it sorted and tidy up that pension problem. A good financial planner will consolidate what you have and give you more control and knowledge of your investments. They can also ensure the pension is well invested, growing and has competitive charges/fees.

You won't believe the number of people who leave significant sums with previous employers. I regularly see clients with old pensions of €100,000 gathering dust. I highly doubt they'd wilfully neglect a rucksack filled with the same amount of cash. For whatever reason, abandoning pensions is commonplace.

If this person is you, get in touch with *questions@askpaul.ie*.

Quiz

Which of the following statements are true?

1. Pensions are guaranteed to provide a comfortable income during retirement.
2. You can only contribute to one pension scheme at a time.
3. A personal pension is only necessary for individuals who don't receive the state pension.
4. Pensions require careful monitoring and adjustment to meet changing financial needs over time.

> Yes, the only true statement is 4. Pensions really require careful monitoring and adjustment to meet changing financial needs over time. Please see a planner.

At what age can I access my pension?

If you are unfortunate enough to experience a terminal illness, then you can access your personal pension at any age under certain circumstances.

Some occupational pension schemes allow you to draw down when you turn fifty. 'Draw down' refers to taking a 25% lump sum from the pension (up to €200,000 tax free with the balance at 20%). Any withdrawal after the lump sum in treated as income and taxable. The balance of the money can sit in an Approved Retirement Fund until you turn sixty. You do not need to draw any money from the remaining fund if you do not wish to.

Otherwise, the earliest age when you may take retirement benefits from a personal pension or PRSA is sixty. From sixty years of age, you must draw down at least 4% from the fund. From seventy, you must draw down 5%. However, you must start using all your retirement benefits by age seventy-five.

This can be good news for many people with multiple pensions from different companies or occupations. The good news is that you don't need to access all these pensions at one time. You can stage them.

Let's take Joe, who has four different employer pension plans. His pensions are worth €150,000, €140,000, €60,000 and €45,000. Joe's total pension pot is €395,000. Joe must 'retire his pension' by seventy-five years of age. By this, I mean he must take his tax-free lump sum from the pension (see below) and start to draw down income from all these funds by the time he's seventy-five.

But Joe doesn't have to take all €395,000 at once unless he wants to. He might not need it all at once. For example, he can take the €150,000 sum at sixty-five while still working part-time. He can 'retire' his other pensions at a later date. The beauty of this strategy is that his pensions can continue to grow tax free. Hopefully, this increases the overall value of his pensions.

What is the big post-retirement bonus?

Prepare to receive a massive welcome bonus when you reach retirement age. This bonus is a tax-free lump sum of 25% of your pension – 25%. Tax free!

So, if you're a really successful pension saver with a fund of €800,000 at retirement, you get to take out €200,000 of this tax free. This money is yours to spend wisely or on a weekend in Las Vegas. It is entirely yours, and you can do as you see fit.

If you're lucky enough to have a huge €2 million retirement fund and want to take out your maximum 25% allowance, the first €200,000 is tax free, and the surplus €300,000 is taxed at 20%. (Pensions are considered income and are subject to the usual tax rates after the tax-free lump sum.)

The balance of your pension is moved into certain post-retirement vehicles, which I'll come to shortly.

So, not only do you get significant tax breaks while building up your pension, but you also get more tax-free treatment when you retire. Building up a personal pension is a great way to grow your wealth.

What pension schemes are available in the private sector?

Occupational pensions with employer contributions

An occupational pension scheme, where your employer matches your contributions, is a significant benefit. Your pension grows rapidly when your employer matches your salary contributions of 5%–10%.

In a tight labour market, many employers use pension contributions as a benefit to attract employees. However, employers are not obliged to offer you a company pension scheme with joint contributions. It's believed to be only a matter of time before employers will be compelled to make a pension contribution for all their employees – in the meantime, it is only a benefit or a perk of some jobs.

Of course, you can add more to your pension to compensate for this. Get some advice.

Standard Personal Retirement Savings Accounts

Employers don't have to contribute to your pension, but they are legally required to provide their employees with access to a pension plan.

They must offer a pension savings account called a Personal Retirement Savings Account (PRSA). If you opt to save in this plan, the employers also must process the pension contribution using the company payroll.

These standard PRSAs have a maximum charge of 5% on each contribution and a 1% a year management fee on the funds.

If this is your only pension option at work, explore alternative options like a personal pension or individual PRSA. The costs of a personal pension or individual PRSA can be better than the terms available under the mandatory standard PRSA.

You need tailored advice if you have no pension provision and earn a decent salary in the private sector. I spend half of my financial planning schedule on pensions advice alone.

Defined benefit pension schemes

Some employers provide a defined benefit (DB) pension and others a defined contribution (DC) pension. Some companies have a hybrid of both.

DB schemes are like the pensions provided to semi-state or public-sector individuals. They promise members pension benefits at normal retirement age based on their salary and service with the employer. These schemes are not very common any more, but they can be valuable. They may or may not be integrated with the state pension.

The employee becomes a member of the scheme and usually makes a fixed contribution as a set percentage of salary. The employer's contribution increases or reduces as needed.

A DB scheme is not a guaranteed pension. It's a promise to pay an individual a pension set out in the scheme's rules. It is the employer's responsibility to ensure that the scheme is adequately funded to meet the scheme's promised benefits. Not all employers have been responsible. A growing number of defined benefit schemes have fallen into difficulty and insolvency.

A DB pension is based on someone's 'final salary', but final salary can be defined as many things. It can be your final salary or your salary less an allowance for the state pension. It can also be based on a career average salary or career average salary less an allowance for the state pension.

The DB pension scheme can also be rigid. It is usually only payable for your lifetime, and many of these pensions die with you. Many employers are closing DB schemes because of onerous administration and costs. When a DB scheme is wound up, the members receive all benefits accrued when the scheme is closed, however all benefits are subject to reduction if the scheme is insolvent. Members who have left or have yet to retire from a DB scheme should review their options. With consent from the trustees a member can convert their DB entitlement to a DC scheme which gives them total control over risk, options to retire early without actuarial reduction, potential to access a higher lump sum at retirement and ensures the capital value of their DB pension will pass to their estate before and after their retirement should they pass away. I can't stress how important it is to have a DB scheme impartially assessed if you have left the scheme.

Defined contribution pension schemes

Defined contribution schemes are based on the contributions paid rather than on the final salary and years of service. Your contributions and the employer's contributions are invested, and the proceeds are used to buy a pension.

Membership of the scheme is conditional on the employee paying the agreed percentage salary rate. Employers will generally match members' contributions up to a certain level, typically 5% of their basic salary.

The most significant advantages of the defined contribution scheme over the defined benefit pension are:

- You have greater control and flexibility over the capital in the fund after retirement.
- It provides the option to invest in an Approved Retirement Fund (ARF). (See more details about the ARF below.) If the person dies, the total value of the ARF passes to their spouse or into their estate if they are single.

Personal pension or retirement annuity contract

The Retirement Annuity Contract (RAC) is better known as a personal pension. Any worker can take out a personal pension. You can buy an RAC directly from life-assurance companies and through brokers and financial planners.

An RAC provides tax relief and all the benefits of a pension at retirement. Unlike the standard PRSA, there are no maximum charges for RACs, so get advice.

CLIENT CASE
BRIAN, AGED 62

Brian is a new client who only arrived to us recently. He worked for a company which has recently changed hands. 'Work has become very stressful', were his first words. He wanted to sort out his pensions, which were all with different companies. He explained he planned to continue working full-time until his mortgage was paid off in a year. Then he said he would apply for a three-day week and try to make it to retirement that way.

When I examined his various pensions, I discovered he had a fund of nearly €800,000. I looked at my very stressed client and said, 'Why are you still working?'

It turned out Brian didn't realise the value of his pensions. He also didn't know he could access some of his pension before he turned sixty-six. He was losing his marbles trying to work to state pension age for no reason.

He will be able to leave work almost immediately. The tax-free lump sum from his pension will clear the last €50,000 he owed on his mortgage. He will also have enough remaining cash left from his lump sum, after clearing his mortgage, to survive on until reaching age sixty-six.

The man left our offices with a massive weight off his shoulders. He has three incredible years ahead rather than three miserable years because he came into our offices to consolidate his pensions.

What are your pension options at retirement?

When you retire, you may take a 25% tax-free lump sum from the pension, as we've discussed. Then, you transfer all or some of your retirement fund into an annuity or other approved scheme that will give you a regular pension income.

An annuity

An annuity is a financial product offered by life assurance and insurance companies. It involves converting your pension fund into a regular income stream for the rest of your life. The annuity provider assumes the investment risk and guarantees a fixed income for the rest of your life.

Your fund's size determines the income received from the annuity. Your age when buying the annuity and the prevailing interest rates will affect the calculations too.

Annuities have been ignored as viable pension options because they have offered low incomes in the low-interest environment of the past fifteen years. Interest is rising now, and annuities are becoming popular again.

The annuity ceases as soon as you die, without any further payment due to your estate, unless you opt for a more expensive joint-life annuity with your spouse.

An Approved Retirement Fund

An Approved Retirement Fund (ARF) is a post-retirement option which enables you to control your pension funds and make investment decisions.

Instead of converting the pension fund into an annuity, you invest the funds in various assets, such as stocks, bonds, cash, property, etc. However, you assume the investment risk. The returns on your investment will impact the fund's value and the income you'll receive. However, you have the flexibility to withdraw money from the ARF when you want.

ARFs, most importantly, are fully transferrable to your spouse on your death in retirement. If your spouse predeceases you at the time of your death in retirement, the assets of the ARF are payable to your estate.

Remember, funds withdrawn from your ARF are subject

to income tax. This makes post-retirement financial planning extremely important, especially if you have multiple pensions and other assets to consider at retirement age.

A lifetime loan mortgage

If you are aged over sixty and are mortgage-free, you also have the option of getting a lifetime loan on your home to raise cash.

This form of equity release is a cash loan on the value of your house and may be a solution if you need money but want to stay in your home. For example, it may come in handy if you run out of money in your pension.

Lifetime loans do not require you to repay this mortgage during your lifetime. Instead, interest is applied to the loan which is repaid after you die, and your house is sold.

See the section on Mortgages where I discuss this option in more depth.

The final word on pensions

Never has a competent financial planner been more important to you than when making retirement decisions. If you make the wrong decisions when you retire, you can make a costly mistake that cannot be reversed.

Although far from perfect, annuities or ARFs can provide a reasonable blend of flexibility and in-built security for retirees – but deciding on which route to take is a big decision.

Your pension is a product of a life's savings and hard-fought wins. When deciding on your pension options at retirement, seek sound financial advice. You will only do this once, so do it right.

This section aims to help you better understand and navigate the complex world of pensions and retirement planning. It also outlines the hazards that may await us in retirement and emphasises the importance of taking control and laying the foundations of our future.

Most of all, I hope you see the importance of seeking good financial advice when facing choices that will affect the rest of your life.

PENSION TERMS AND THEIR MEANINGS

- **PRB (Personal Retirement Bond):** A DIY pension savings pot. If you leave a job where you had a pension, you can transfer your pension savings into a PRB. This way, you manage your own pension instead of leaving it with your old employer.
- **PRSA (Personal Retirement Savings Account):** This is a pension scheme designed for individuals who do not have access to an occupational pension. It enables you to contribute money on your own terms.
- **ARF (Approved Retirement Fund):** This is like a post-retirement piggy bank. ARFs are investment funds that individuals can choose to transfer their pension funds into upon retirement. The money in an ARF is invested, and you can draw regular or occasional income from it as needed.
- **AVC (Additional Voluntary Contributions):** These are extra contributions that individuals can make to their workplace pension scheme. If you contribute

more to your pension savings than the minimum required, you get a bigger pension pot at the end.

- **PPP (Personal Pension Plan)**: This is an individual pension plan that you can set up on your own. It's like a saving scheme for self-employed people or employees not covered by a company pension scheme. It enables you to save for your retirement and get tax relief on your contributions.

Your 7-point action plan for your retirement

- Decide what age you want to stop working.
- Decide what you want to do when you retire.
- Know how much you will need month to month to live.
- Check your spouse's or partner's financial position for their retirement.
- Consider if you have specific care needs in retirement.
- If you have a pension in place, check the funding and consider if it is enough for what you need.
- If you have no financial plan in place, how much longer can you leave it?

Acknowledgements

I want to send special thanks to you, the reader, for choosing to buy this book. I sincerely hope that this book has inspired you to take positive action in your financial life and future. My ultimate aim with *Money Made Easy* is to empower you in your relationship with money and set you on the path of financial well-being. I hope you continue the journey with me by following the askpaul.ie social media channels along with signing up to my monthly newsletter on www.askpaul.ie. You can also book in for various financial planning consultations with us by visiting the website.

I also want to express gratitude to the professionals I've had the privilege to work with over the past twenty years. Thanks especially to Conor Byrne, my longest-standing colleague. You've been with me from the start and your guidance, professional support and friendship have been invaluable.

I also want to thank too many others to list, but include colleagues from my company origins as Pax Asset Management to askpaul and now Fairstone. I'm also truly grateful to Paul Kelly, who burned the midnight oil to help me meet the deadline for this book.

A huge thanks to my publishers Hachette Ireland and to the team there, especially to Ciara Doorley and Kathryn Rogers for their help.

Most of all, I wish to extend my heartfelt appreciation for the unwavering trust that you, our clients, have placed in me over the last two decades. What they teach you in college will get you so far, but it's your unique lives, aspirations and financial goals that have provided a priceless education. Constant engagement with you and your families continues to fuel my passion for my career.

I feel very lucky. Enhancing people's financial wellness and security is my dream job. I look forward to continuing to serve everyone's financial planning needs long into the future!

Resources and Sources

Aviva Risk Check Calculator (https://tools.friendsfirst.ie/prc)

Central Credit Register (centralcreditregister.ie)

Competition and Consumer Protection Commission (ccpc.ie)

Consumer Financial Protection Bureau (consumerfinance.gov)

Credit Union (creditunion.ie)

daft.ie

Financial Planning Standards Board (www.fpsb.ie)

First Home Scheme (firsthomescheme.ie)

Health Insurance Authority (hia.ie)

iReach Insights (ireachhq.com)

Money Advice and Budgeting Service (mabs.ie)

MyWelfare (mywelfare.ie)

National Treasury Management Agency (ntma.ie)

Revenue Commissioners (revenue.ie)

St Vincent de Paul (svp.ie)

Total Health Cover (totalhealthcover.ie)

Index

O

occupational pensions 290, 305–308
online trading platforms 122
overdrafts 96–97

P

Pay As You Earn (PAYE) 153
pensions 279–313
  accessing 303–304
  auto-enrolment 293–294
  definition 280–281, 312–313
  forgotten 300–302
  number of 283–284
  occupational pensions 290, 305–308
  personal pensions 290–291
  Personal Retirement Savings
    Account 299, 305–306
  post-retirement 296–297, 304,
    309–311
  private pensions 295–296
  public-service pensions 291–292
  starting 298
  state pensions 288–289, 296–297
  tax on contributions 167, 295–296
  time bomb 284–288
  types of 288–292
  why they are needed 281–282
  women and 287–288
personal budgeting 37–72
Personal Contract Plans 95–96
Personal Insolvency Practitioner
  (PIP) 78
personal loans 98–100
personal pensions 290–291
Personal Retirement Savings Account
  (PRSA) 299, 305–306
private health insurance 208–215
  comparing policies 210–213
  definition 208
  providers 209
private pensions 295–296
problem debt 23
property 127–131
property funds, *see investment funds*

protection gap 219–221
public-service pensions 291–292

R

retail investors 122–124
Revolving debt 94
risk intolerance 115–116

S

saving 105–109, 300, *see also investing*
  difference to investing 111–112
  interest 112–115
  mortgages 247, 269–270
savings challenge 44–45
second-time house buyers 250–251
Section 72 172–173, 217–218
secured debt 94
serious-illness cover 185, 188–190,
  201–202
setting goals 82
shares 131–134
short-term debt 55–57
specified serious-illness cover 199–200
stamp duty 154, 258
state pension 288–289, 296–297
stockbrokers 121
stocks 131–134
St Vincent de Paul 77

T

talking about money 22, 23–24
taxes 149–178
  advisors 155–156
  and businesses 169–171
  and politics 154–155
  Capital Acquisitions Tax 171–173
  Capital Gains Tax 173–174
  collection 152–154, 156
  corporation tax 153
  customs duty 154